Addressing Ethnic Profiling by Police

A Report on the Strategies for Effective Police Stop and Search Project

Improving relations between police and minority communities by increasing the fairness, effectiveness, and accountability of police stops in Bulgaria, Hungary, and Spain

AGIS 2006

OPEN SOCIETY INSTITUTE
NEW YORK

Copyright © 2009 by the Open Society Institute. All rights reserved.

No part of this publication may be reproduced, stored in a retrieval system, or transmitted in any form or by any means without the prior permission of the publisher.

ISBN: 978-1-891385-89-6

Published by
Open Society Institute
400 West 59th Street
New York, NY 10019 USA
www.soros.org

For more information contact:
Open Society Justice Initiative
400 West 59th Street
New York, NY 10019 USA
www.justiceinitiative.org

Cover designed by Judit Kovács | Createch Ltd.
Cover photo by Javier Soriano | AFP | Getty Images
Text layout and printing by Createch Ltd.

Table of Contents

Acknowledgments		5
I.	Executive Summary and Recommendations	9
II.	What is Ethnic Profiling and How Did STEPSS Address It?	17
III.	Explaining Stop Patterns: Key Terms and Concepts	23
IV.	STEPSS Data Analysis and Results	27
V.	The STEPSS Process	55
VI.	Conclusions	77
VII.	Annexes	
	A Police Powers to Conduct Stops in STEPSS Partner Countries	79
	B Hungarian Sampling Design and Methodological Issues	83
	C STEPSS Resource Packet	87
	D Ethnic Profiling in Europe: An Overview of the Justice Initiative Project	89
Notes		91

Acknowledgments

The Strategies for Effective Police Stop and Search (STEPSS) project would not have been possible without the dedication, insight and hard work of many people, not all of whom can be thanked individually. The Open Society Justice Initiative nevertheless wishes to acknowledge the contributions of the following persons and institutions:

Bulgaria
STEPSS was coordinated by the Ministry of the Interior, the Center for the Study of Democracy (CSD), and the Open Society Institute–Sofia. We thank Philip Gounev, Chavdar Chervenkov, and Tihomir Bezlov of CSD; Maria Metodieva and Kamelia Dimitrova of OSI–Sofia; Milcho Enev, Plamen Petkov, Iliana Ivanova-Sapundzhicva, Vyacheslav Evogiev of the General Directorate of Police; Albena Haralampieva and Julian Pishev (interpreters); and community representatives Dimitar Georgiev and Dancho Panayotov (Sofia), Krasimir Asenov (Plovdiv), Zarko Ognianov and Sema Asenova (Haskovo).

Hungary
STEPSS was coordinated by the Hungarian Helsinki Committee (HHC), National Police Headquarters, and the Hungarian Police College. We thank Balázs Tóth, András Kádár, Zsófia Moldova of HHC; Júlia Kömer (independent sociologist), Éva Lukásevich, László Zélity, Sándor Mergancz, András Kiss, Ildikó Salacz, and Róbert Plánk of the Hungarian

National Police; Zsolt Németh of the Police College; and civilian monitors Jenő Setét (Budapest), Imre Bogdán (Kaposvár), and Zsolt Virág (Szeged); and Erzsébet Czapp (interpreter).

Spain

STEPSS was coordinated by the Grupo de Estudios y Alternativas 21 (GEA 21), the Municipal Police of Girona, the Municipal Police of Fuenlabrada, the Mossos d'Esquadra regional police of Catalunya, the Police College of Catalunya, the Institute for Police Studies, the Spanish National Police, and the UNESCO Center of Catalunya. We thank Daniel Wagman, Maggie Schmitt, and Begoña Pernas of GEA 21; Eduard Sallent Peña, Yvonne Valero i Martínez, and Rosa Negre of the Mossos d'Esquadra; Josep Palouzié i Vizcaya of the Municipal Police of Girona; Ignasi López i Cleville of the Municipal Police of Olot; Lola Valles of the Police College of Catalunya; Jose Francisco Cano de la Vega and David Martin of the Municipal Police of Fuenlabrada; Pedro Luis Canales of the Police Academy of Madrid; Silvia Cedó Lluis and Saloua L'Aouiji Gharbi of the UNESCO Center of Catalunya, Mohamed Najih of the Sergi Foundation, Amadou Sam Daff of the Coordination of Senegalese Associations; Mimoun Amrioui of the Islamic Center of Fuenlabrada; Javier Ramirez of SOS Racismo; and Chema Garcia of Amnesty International of Spain.

United Kingdom

The technical support of U.K. partners was invaluable. For their time and willingness to share their experiences—both good and bad—we thank the Ministry of Justice of England and Wales, the London Metropolitan Police Service (MPS), and the Leicestershire Constabulary. We are especially grateful to Mike Ainsworth and Tim Maile of the Ministry of Justice; Nicholas Jupp, Ted Henderson, Geoff Bishop, Raj Kohli, Vic Olisa, Andy Walker, Stef Morris, David Maguire, Hywel Williams, Adrian Lowes, and Les Bowles of the MPS; Charlene Brown, Robi Chowdry, and Saad Butt of the Metropolitan Police Service Youth Independent Advisory Group; Richard Keenan, Nick Glynn, Amrik Basra, Ian Coulton, Craig Baker, and Pete Bumpus of the Leicestershire Constabulary; Suleman Nagdi of the Federation of Muslim Organisations-Leicester; Julie Sykes of the West Yorkshire Constabulary; Neil Franklin of the Crown Prosecution Service West Yorkshire; Ebrahim Dockrat of the West Yorkshire Race Scrutiny Panel; Charlie Hedges of the National Policing Improvement Agency; Mary John-Bapiste and Nathan Winch of the Greater London Authority; Mike Franklin of the Independent Police Complaints Commission; Iqbal Bhana of the Community Panel; Mark Fearon of the Lambeth Youth Council. Thanks also to the many officers and community members in London and Leicester who met with us and took us on ride-alongs.

Additional thanks to Mike Ainsworth of the Ministry of Justice, Mike Shiner of the London School of Economics, and Joel Miller of the Vera Institute of Justice in New York, for help reviewing the stop data.

We are particularly grateful to the European Commission's AGIS Programme for their generous grant in support of the STEPSS project.

This report was written by Rebekah Delsol, project officer for the Justice Initiative's Ethnic Profiling in Europe project, on the basis of country reports prepared by the coordinators in Bulgaria, Hungary, and Spain. It was edited by Rachel Neild, Indira Goris, James Goldston, Robert Varenik, Rachel Hart, and David Berry.

I. Executive Summary and Recommendations

The term "ethnic profiling" describes the use by law enforcement officers of race, ethnicity, religion, or national origin rather than individual behavior as the basis for making decisions about who has been or may be involved in criminal activity. Ethnic profiling appears most frequently in police officers' decisions about who to stop and ask for identity papers (ID), question, search, and sometimes arrest. Although ethnic profiling is widespread,[1] the practice has not been sufficiently studied. Ethnic profiling constitutes discrimination and thus breaches fundamental human rights norms, but it has not been expressly outlawed by any European government. Profiling is also counterproductive. It misdirects law enforcement resources and alienates some of the very people whose cooperation is necessary for effective crime detection.

Ethnic profiling may result from the intentional racism of individual police officers, but is frequently the cumulative result of unconscious and unchecked ethnic stereotypes. It can also reflect institutional factors, such as police deployment patterns that do not reflect overt racial animus, but nonetheless have disparate impacts on minorities. Stop and search powers are a basic tool of policing and the primary point of contact with police for most people; yet their impact and effectiveness are rarely examined.

Over 18 months, starting in January 2007, the Open Society Justice Initiative worked with police forces and civil society organizations in Bulgaria, Hungary, and Spain to monitor the use of police stops in a project supported by the European Commission's AGIS Programme titled "Strategies for Effective Police Stop and Search project," or STEPSS. The participating organizations and individuals not only had the foresight to recognize that they might have a problem with ethnic profiling, but were also willing to tackle the issue directly and share their experiences.

The STEPSS project was a three-country initiative designed to improve police-minority relations through the more accountable and effective use of police powers in selected communities. Through the project, participating police forces developed tools to monitor the use of identity checks and stop and search powers, to determine whether they affect minority communities in a disproportionate manner, and to enable an analysis of their effectiveness in detecting and investigating crime.

STEPSS project activities included an audit of current policies, practices, and training; a study tour of several sites in England; development of new guidelines, training methods, and a monitoring tool; and the monitoring of stops and ID checks for a period of six months. Community consultation was integral to each step of the project process, with the monitoring results used to further police-community discussion of public safety policies and resource allocation, and to support the development, where necessary, of alternative approaches to local crime and safety problems.

STEPSS aimed to improve police relations with minority communities through:

- Improving police training, operational and legal guidance, and the supervision of ID checks, stops, and searches.
- Developing a monitoring system that enhances police management of and accountability for stops.
- Creating a forum and increasing minority communities' ability to participate in dialogue with the police and set local policing priorities
- Creating replicable models of good practice that can be disseminated regionally.

STEPSS undertook an assessment of existing policy and practice, designed forms for recording stops, prepared and trained officers on operational protocols, and collected stop data for six months in pilot sites in each country. Throughout the process, police met with local community groups to share and discuss the stop data. The data revealed that police were engaging in ethnic profiling. In every pilot site, police were profiling people based on ethnicity or national origin. Minorities were more likely to be stopped, often more likely to be searched, but, almost without exception, were no more likely to be found to be offending than the majority group. In some cases, they were significantly less likely to be found offending than ethnic majority residents—but were subjected to profiling, nonetheless.

The data also clearly showed that specific operations and types of deployment led to more ethnic profiling. When officers had greater discretion to make stops, minorities were stopped at an increasingly disproportionate rate. Requiring officers to gather stop data and record their grounds for the stop reduced discretion and increased the effectiveness of officers' use of stops. In both Hungary and Spain, officers in the STEPSS project tended to make fewer stops over the period that they were required to record stops, but the proportion of stops that produced an arrest or other positive law enforcement outcome increased. When officers focus on developing clear and individualized grounds for stops, and are held accountable by supervisors, they are more effective.

Before reviewing the country data, it is important to note that some amount of ethnic profiling across European Union (EU) member states is driven by the domestic enforcement of immigration law. Indeed, in Spain the Constitutional Court has ruled that police officers may use ethnicity as a factor in making decisions about immigration enforcement.[2] Immigration enforcement does not, however, play a significant role in explaining the results of the STEPSS data gathering. While some police stops in Hungary and Bulgaria, may have been motivated by immigration concerns (as each country had a pilot site near the border), the number of immigrants and non-Roma minorities in the two countries is extremely small and barely appears in the STEPSS data. Immigration enforcement is a more pressing issue in Spain where large-scale migration is a recent and ongoing phenomenon. The Spanish National Police enforce immigration law; the municipal police and Mossos d'Esquadra (Catalan regional police) only do so at the request of national police authorities and were not conducting such operations during the period of STEPSS data gathering. Hence, for the purposes of the STEPSS project, the results were not affected by the reality that, in enforcing immigration law, as opposed to criminal law, relevant authorities may generally target their investigative activities at non-citizens. Rather, any targeting of immigrants indicated by project data raises a red flag, because, for the purposes of enforcing criminal law, police generally have no reasonable basis for assuming that immigrants (like ethnic minorities) are more or less likely to commit crimes than anyone else. The question of immigration enforcement is nonetheless a serious one for any police service that may wish to introduce stop forms while also engaged in enforcing immigration controls. In this case, the data from stop forms could provide useful insights into the degree to which immigration does in fact drive profiling of legal immigrants, and how effective such operations are in terms of identifying illegal migrants when weighed against the burden of their impact on legal immigrants and minority-origin citizens.

Country and Pilot Site Results

Throughout Hungary, Roma[3] are three times more likely to be stopped by police than non-Roma, yet the rate at which each group is detected in the commission of an offense is almost identical. The disparity in the stop rate is particularly disturbing given that Hungarian police conduct massive numbers of stops: as many as 325 per 1,000 residents in one pilot site, 65 per 1,000 and 93 per 1,000 in the other two, compared to an average of 29 per 1,000 in the two Spanish STEPSS sites, and 39 stops and 20 stops and searches per 1,000 in the United Kingdom.[4] The stop data clearly showed that Hungarian officers' stops are not detecting crime: only one percent of their stops lead to arrest; two percent lead to short-term arrest,[5] and 18 percent to petty offense procedures being instigated (a broad category of minor administrative infractions and misdemeanors). Large numbers of people are inconvenienced by police stops with little result, and those people are disproportionately Roma. However, during the STEPSS project, officers in the Budapest and Szeged pilot areas significantly decreased their use of stops; this drop was accompanied by an increase in the rate at which stops produced results.

In Spain, some ethnic minority groups were stopped more than others, but all ethnic minorities were stopped more—sometimes far more—than ethnic Spaniards.[6] In Girona, the municipal police stopped Moroccans 6.7 times more often than Spaniards, and Romanians 10 times more often. Yet they only detected offenses in nine percent of stops of Moroccans compared to 17 percent of stops of ethnic Spaniards and 19 percent of stops of Romanians. The Mossos d'Esquadra (the regional police that also patrols Girona) not only stopped ethnic groups more often (Romanians were stopped 6.1 times more often, and Moroccans 10 times more often than Spaniards), they also searched ethnic minorities at highly disproportionate rates (70 percent of Moroccans stopped and 77 percent of Romanians who were stopped were searched, compared to 52 percent of Spaniards). Only in the case of Romanians does this discrepancy appear to have some basis, as the police detected offenses slightly more frequently (17 percent of the time compared to eight percent for Spaniards and 11 percent for Moroccans). The overall picture is one of disproportionate treatment of ethnic minority groups with little or no basis in greater police efficiency.

In Fuenlabrada, the second Spanish pilot site, the municipal police had rates of disproportionality similar to those in Girona at the start of the project. Over the six months of data gathering, the police in Fuenlabrada reduced the disproportionality in the rate at which they were stopping all persons of immigrant origin. They achieved a dramatic decrease in stops of Moroccans from 9.6 times more often than Spaniards to 3.4 times more often, largely because they ended a fruitless counter-terror operation. Furthermore, the rate at which officers conducted stops overall fell by well over half, while the percentage of their stops that produced positive outcomes increased by nearly three times. Fuenlabrada's police managers and supervisors achieved these remarkable results by making systemic use of the STEPSS data both for closer supervision of individual patrol officers and for force-wide management of operations and personnel deployment. The data enabled them to factor disproportionate ethnic impacts into their strategic decision-making and reduce unfair policing while enhancing efficiency.

Unfortunately, in Bulgaria, insufficient support from mid-level police managers—despite the commitment of national police leaders—and flaws in project implementation meant that not enough data were gathered to be statistically valid. The STEPSS experience in Bulgaria nonetheless offers valuable lessons in the challenges that data-driven police reform initiatives face. Challenges were also confronted in other pilot sites in Hungary and Spain. These challenges include the difficulty of achieving the "buy-in" and commitment of officers from every level of the force; the challenges of working with local community organizations; as well as more technical difficulties involving the design of stop forms, data entry, and training. Although ethnic data collection is a controversial concept in most European Union member states, where many governments argue that data protection standards preclude the collection of information on ethnicity and policing, the national data protection authorities in the participating countries reviewed and approved of the stop forms and the systems for storing ethnic statistics, finding that they did not violate EU or national standards.

Proponents of ethnic profiling claim that it is simply part of "good policing" and crime prevention, because minority groups are more likely to be involved in crime. Corroborating other studies, STEPSS demonstrates that this is simply not true. Previous studies suggest that profiling is ineffective and even counterproductive.[7] Police need to have legitimacy in the eyes of citizens. People must have confidence that the police will act fairly and effectively within the law. One of the most gratifying results of STEPSS was the discussions and new relationships forged through the police-community groups and civilian engagement in monitoring police stops. In Fuenlabrada, these discussions directly helped the municipal police in identifying and addressing crime patterns and other community concerns. In Hungary, where the project used regular "ride-alongs" to monitor the data gathering, the police and Roma representatives developed new understandings and insights; one unanticipated outcome is that one of the Roma STEPSS participants has now joined the police force.

The United Kingdom and the United States have grappled with disproportionality in stop and search or racial profiling (in the terminology of each setting) over decades and continue to do so. Beyond the basic issue of recognizing that police use of stop and search may have a discriminatory impact on ethnic minorities, understanding and changing the factors that drive ethnic profiling is a complex undertaking involving culture and practice, institutions and communities. STEPSS project partners undertook an ambitious series of activities over a short project timespan; they have helped to deepen our understanding of the dynamics of ethnic profiling and the ways in which it may be addressed. These achievements, and the challenges faced along the way, have produced valuable lessons both for the pilot sites continuing this work and for others adopting and adapting the STEPSS approach.

STEPSS shows that, while it is not easy, it is possible, even in a short period of time, to identify and begin to address patterns of disproportionality—and that doing so does not jeopardize safety. Indeed it enhances the efficiency and effectiveness with which officers use stop and search powers. The challenge ahead is to build upon and deepen the use of stop data to strengthen community-police consultation and institutionalize results-based management of the use of stops, including examining disproportionality, effectiveness, and the quality of encounters.

Recommendations[8]

The following recommendations address national and local political authorities as well as police managers regarding the need to recognize ethnic profiling and address it through changes in police policies and practices. Further recommendations on the use of ethnic data gathering as a key tool for monitoring discrimination and establishing fair and effective policing are directed to civil society and community leaders. These recommendations are complemented by boxes with specific lessons from the STEPSS project, described in Chapter IV.

To national political authorities:

1. Speak out against discrimination in all its forms, including ethnic profiling. Political leaders at all levels play an important role in shaping public opinion and should use their authority to speak out against discrimination and ethnic profiling.

2. Review laws and operational guidelines establishing and regulating police powers and, where necessary, strengthen non-discrimination standards and practices. Law and operational guidance should establish clear and precise standards for initiating and conducting stops, identity checks, and searches, including their function and grounds for carrying them out. Stops should be based upon a reasonable individualized suspicion that the subject in question has committed or is in the act of committing a crime. Law and/or police operational guidelines should clarify the nature of "suspicion" and state categorically that ethnicity and other personal characteristics may not constitute the reason for a stop (in the absence of a specific suspect description).

3. Create robust public-complaint mechanisms if they are not already well-established, preferably including specialized independent oversight or control mechanisms. Civilian oversight can enhance the legitimacy of the complaints process and improve policing by identifying problematic practices.

To police authorities and managers:

4. Reach out to ethnic and religious minority communities through public forums and discussion to enhance mutual understanding and trust; develop community-policing initiatives; and create specialized ethnic and religious outreach units in the police, among other approaches.

5. Recruit candidates from immigrant or minority groups to create a police service representative of the community that it serves. Complement minority recruitment with policies that support institutional non-discrimination and minority retention.

6. Avoid using using explicit information about ethnic origin in public statements unless it is directly relevant and necessary. In the release of information about crimes, there is generally no need to discuss the ethnicity of victims or perpetrators; all such reports should treat all subjects equally. In releasing statistics on crime rates, arrests, and other policing matters, it is important for police to be ethnically neutral, to avoid creating unwarranted associations between immigrants, minorities, and crime. For example, arrests on immigration grounds should be recorded separately from arrests on non-immigration grounds. Implement a monitoring system to record stops and ethnicity in order to detect and address any patterns of disproportionality and increase the effectiveness of officers' use of stops.

7. Verify that ethnic data collection complies with personal data protection standards. Stop forms and protocols must be reviewed by national data protection bodies.

8. Analyze stop data on a regular basis and in consultation with the community, to maximize the value of the data for police supervision and management.

9. Share stop data with the community. Police should establish regular consultations with community members, particularly those from minority groups, as a regular institutional policy. Such meetings can increase police accountability to the community, and can also aid in gathering information on crime problems, settling local policing priorities, and finding solutions to crime and other community concerns.

10. Review and, if necessary, strengthen the supervision of patrol officers' use of stops and searches, to determine if the stops and searches are fair and effective; managers should also use stop forms to check the reasons officers give for making stops, as well as their conduct during stops.

11. Train police managers in using stop form data to supervise officers' use of identity checks, stops, and searches. (See chart in Chapter V for further details on management and supervision uses of stop form data.)

12. Give all police officers practical training on the use of stop and search powers, including a discussion of the influence of negative stereotypes, and guidance on the need to focus on suspicious behaviors rather than appearance.

13. Complement data gathering with steps to assure courteous treatment of all members of the public during police stops. Clear standards, training, and supervision will improve officer conduct during stops. Compliance with established standards should be enhanced or enforced through mechanisms that obtain feedback from citizens (such as comment boxes, surveys sampling persons stopped, and qualitative monitoring through community consultative groups or youth outreach programs).

To civil society and community leaders:

14. Advocate for policies that promote non-discrimination in policing.

15. Study police-community relations and the use of police powers to build understanding of the dynamics of disproportionality and support the development of policies and initiatives in response.

16. Engage in dialogue with police and political authorities, to build trust and understanding.

17. Support efforts by police to monitor identity checks and stops and searches; demand that statistical data be shared to support joint assessment of policing tactics and local security priorities.

II. What is Ethnic Profiling and How Did STEPSS Address It?

The term "ethnic profiling" refers to the use of race, ethnicity, religion, or national origin rather than individual behavior as the basis for making law enforcement decisions about who may be involved in criminal activity. Ethnic profiling appears most frequently in law enforcement officers' decisions about who to stop and ask for identify papers, question, search, and sometimes arrest. Carrying out identity checks and stops and searches is one of the most basic tools of policing, yet their use, their impact, and their efficiency are rarely examined.[9]

There is little clarity or consensus in Europe today about what constitutes ethnic profiling and even less about how to address it. Specific definitions of ethnic profiling vary along a continuum ranging from the intentional use of race alone to the conscious or unconscious use of race along with other factors as the reason for the stop. Narrow definitions say that ethnic profiling occurs when officers make the decision to stop *solely* on the basis of a person's perceived ethnicity. The narrow definition of ethnic profiling fails to capture the reality of policing on the streets during which officers base decisions on a number of factors that may include or be related to a person's perceived ethnicity. Ethnic profiling may be caused by the purposefully racist behavior of individual officers, but it may also result from the unconscious use of racist stereotypes, and it can reflect institutional factors such as unequal enforcement of the law or deployment patterns that have a disparate impact on ethnic minority groups.

Ethnic profiling is distinct from "criminal profiling," which relies on statistical categorizations based on identifiable characteristics believed to correlate with certain behaviors, such as serial killer, hijacker, or drug courier profiles that have been developed. Ethnicity is frequently and properly used to compile "suspect profiles" or suspect descriptions, generally based on a witness description of a person connected with a particular crime committed at a specific time and place.

Proponents of ethnic profiling claim that it is simply part of "good policing" and crime prevention as minority groups are more likely to be involved in crime. Corroborating other studies, the data presented in this report demonstrate that this is simply not true. Studies suggest that profiling is ineffective and even counterproductive. Police need to have legitimacy in the eyes of citizens, and people must have confidence that the police will act fairly and effectively within the law. Ethnic profiling is ineffective because it destroys the trust of communities in the police and reduces their willingness to cooperate in criminal or terrorism investigations or turn to the police to control crime in their neighborhoods. It also exacts a high price on individuals, groups, and communities that are singled out for disproportionate attention. For the individual stopped and detained, the experience can be frightening and humiliating. Ethnic profiling also serves to stigmatize whole groups as "suspect communities," contributing to the over-representation of ethnic minorities in other parts of the criminal justice system, perpetuating negative stereotypes and legitimizing racism.

Human rights reports and anecdotal evidence suggest that ethnic profiling is widespread in Europe, yet the issue has been subject to little systematic research. In 2005, the Open Society Justice Initiative undertook research with partners in Bulgaria, Hungary, and Spain,[10] using a qualitative approach based on interviews with police officers, focus groups and interviews with Roma in all three countries, and interviews with immigrants in Spain. In Bulgaria and Hungary, the research also included a household survey of peoples' experiences and perception of police use of stops. Despite the very different national contexts, it was clear that police in all three countries were profiling Roma and other minorities. Roma pedestrians in Bulgaria and Hungary and immigrants in Spain were more likely to be stopped than members of the majority population and, once stopped they were more likely to report an unpleasant experience with the police. The interviews also found that officers frequently cited often unobjective and unverifiable factors such as a "sixth sense," or "intuition" or "past experience" as driving their decisions about whom to stop, sometimes adding factors such as a person appearing "nervous," "out of place," or "strange."[11] The research found that while stops may be called in to headquarters, they are generally not reviewed by line supervisors at local stations, nor are they recorded and assessed systematically to measure their efficiency and fairness.

The research in Bulgaria, Hungary, and Spain provided initial insights into ethnic differences in stops. Yet methodological variations in the research—particularly the dearth of data on the ethnicity of those stopped—made it impossible to determine the extent of ethnic profiling taking place. Ethnic statistics are essential to identify discriminatory outcomes, including those that result from policies or patterns of practice that do not necessarily reflect discriminatory intent. The collection of ethnic data is necessary to determine the extent of any profiling, demonstrate its impact on minority groups, and provide effective redress.[12]

To date, the United Kingdom is the only EU member state systematically collecting data on police stops and ethnicity. Data collection has not ended the problem in the United Kingdom—black and Asian British people are still stopped more than whites—but it has provided the basis for open and informed discussion between the police and local communities about the reasons for these disparities, and helped in developing policies to respond to them. Without data gathering, the problem of ethnic profiling is far more likely to go unrecognized, uncharted, and unaddressed.

Building on research and lessons learned from the United Kingdom, the STEPSS project developed tools and processes to monitor police stops. A stop form that included data on the ethnicity of the person stopped was created, and the findings were discussed with committees made up of representatives of local minority communities. Through this process, STEPSS hoped to show that disproportionate stops of minorities (i.e. ethnic profiling) can be reduced without negative consequences for policing, and that police-community relations will be improved as a result. STEPSS was launched in January 2007, and carried out by five police forces over 22 months in eight pilot sites in Spain, Hungary, and Bulgaria. STEPSS project objectives were to:

(1) identify and reduce disproportionality in identity checks and stops and searches of ethnic minority and immigrant communities;
(2) increase the efficiency of police stops through improved management and supervision; and
(3) improve police-community relations by sharing and discussing stop data and reviewing security concerns and operational priorities;
(4) create models of good practice to share with other police forces.

STEPSS undertook the same basic set of activities in each country—with many adaptations to local realities—led by coordination teams composed of police, community, and civil society representatives. The STEPSS process to measure and address ethnic profiling involved:

- auditing of existing law, policies, and practices;
- learning from other police forces, including through a study tour in the United Kingdom and visits by U.K. police officers to pilot sites in Bulgaria, Hungary, and Spain;
- developing new guidelines for the use of stops and searches, including instructions on making stops based on reasonable suspicion;
- developing a stop form and reviewing compliance with national data protection authorities;
- training police officers in the objectives of the project, the concept of ethnic profiling, and the use of stop forms and operational guidance;
- training community members in the same way police officers were trained; in addition, community members also provided training to police on local minority communities and experiences of being stopped;
- using forms to gather data on stops for six months, from October 2007 to April/May 2008;
- sharing stop data on a monthly basis with consultative committees made up of local residents; and
- completing an analysis of all data on stops and presenting the findings of that analysis.

More detail on the project sites is given below.

BULGARIA

Police: Bulgaria has a single national police force under the Ministry of the Interior, made up of various agencies responsible for crime detection and prevention, public order, and control of highway traffic.

STEPSS project sites: Fifth Area Police Department (APD) in the capital Sofia, Third Area Police Department in the city of Plovdiv, and the Area Police Department of the town of Haskovo. The participating police departments were chosen by the Ministry of the Interior, which endeavored to select both small and large towns, with commuting and permanently-resident ethnic minority groups.

Population: The 2001 census registered 6,605,000 ethnic Bulgarians, 747,000 ethnic Turks, and 371,000 Roma. Yet Roma leaders and demographic experts suggest that the number of Roma is much higher, with estimates ranging between 600,000 and 750,000.

HUNGARY

Police: Hungary has a single national police force under the Ministry of Justice and Law Enforcement.

STEPSS project sites: Sixth District Budapest, Szeged, and Kaposvár. These are policing districts with differing populations, crime profiles, and resources. Budapest's Sixth District covers a busy city center that includes Budapest's main railway station and a large retail area; Szeged is a medium sized district on the Romanian border with a population of 200,000; and Kaposvár is a rural district with 120,000 inhabitants.

Population: Hungary has a total population of 10,045,000 of which it is estimated that 620,000 or 6.2 percent are Roma. All other ethnic groups make up less than 0.5 percent of the population.

SPAIN

Police: Spain has two national police forces: the Policía Nacional and the Guardia Civil Española; a regional police force in Catalunya (known as the Mossos d'Esquadra) and in the Basque country; and local, municipal police throughout Spain.

STEPSS project sites: Fuenlabrada (a suburb south of Madrid), and Girona (in Catalunya).

Population: Spain has a total population of 46 million, including 4.5 million foreign residents. Fuenlabrada's total population is 209,102 of whom 15.9 percent are foreigners; Girona's total population is 96,461 of whom 20.7 percent are foreigners.

III. Explaining Stop Patterns: Key Terms and Concepts

In order to understand, measure, and address ethnic profiling by police, it is important to have a common understanding of its chief components. The terms and concepts described here were essential elements of the project's conception.

Numbers of stops: The extent to which police forces use their stop powers varies greatly among police forces, reflecting crime rates, numbers of operational officers, and policing styles. The stop rate is generally presented as the number of stops per 1,000 people in the residential population. In 2006–2007 police forces within England and Wales conducted 39 stops and 20 stops and searches per 1,000 residents.[13]

Measuring Fairness: Fairness is assessed in terms of: (a) disproportionality in the rate at which ethnic minority and majority residents are stopped, in relation to their numbers in the wider population;[14] and (b) the treatment of people once they have been stopped.

Disproportionality is calculated by using police records to measure the rates at which people from ethnic minority groups are stopped, compared to the rates at which the majority group is stopped. The clearest way to understand disproportionality is by using an odds ratio, which can be best understood by the sentence, "black people are X times more likely to be stopped than white people." If stops are being conducted equally against all ethnic groups the ratios would be 1.0 indicating that black people are no more likely to be stopped that white people. Odds ratios between 1.0 and 1.5 are most likely benign; an odds ratio greater than 1.5 indicates ethnic profiling.[15] Evidence of disproportionality does not automatically prove discrimination; the data have to be examined further to look at what patterns emerge and how such patterns might be explained.

For example, the first proven case of racial profiling in the United States, found that black motorists were 4.9 times more likely to be stopped than other drivers by the New Jersey State Police.[16] U.K. statistics for 2006–2007 show that black people were 2.4 times more likely to be stopped than white people, and Asian people were 1.1 times more likely to be stopped.[17] The largest odds ratio documented to date is a study finding that non-Slavs were 21.8 times more likely than Slavs to be stopped on the Moscow Metro.[18]

Police *treatment* of the person they have stopped, or the *quality of the stop*, has been found to be the greatest concern to people stopped.[19] It is challenging to find objective measures of stop quality, but studies have assessed how long stops take, how often they lead to searches, the hit rate (or percentage of stops revealing a crime or other violation), and use of force (such as handcuffs or physical restraints). In the United Kingdom, in 2006–2007, black people were 7.7 times more likely to be searched than white people and Asian people were 2.2 times more likely to be searched than white people.[20] A study of traffic stops in Las Vegas, Nevada, showed that black and Latino people were more likely to be handcuffed and held for longer periods of time during stops.[21]

Effectiveness: The hit rate is a common measure of the effectiveness of stops (sometimes termed productivity). Yet police services do not have a consistent definition of what constitutes a "hit." Consequently, hit data cannot be compared across police jurisdictions without first carefully assessing the types of outcomes that each service considers a hit. The United Kingdom measures arrests resulting from stops and searches, whereas many U.S. jurisdictions include all positive outcomes, including seizure of contraband, administrative or traffic citations, and arrests.[22] It is sometimes said that stops have a disruptive or deterrent effect, and that they have value in allowing intelligence gathering through questioning those stopped; however, research has been unable to determine the extent of these impacts.[23]

It is often argued that ethnic minorities and immigrants are profiled because they offend at higher rates. But data on hit rates from different cities and countries are remarkably consistent in showing that hit rates do not vary significantly by ethnic group. In the United Kingdom, in 2006–2007, the arrest rate for whites and blacks who were stopped was 12 percent, while it was 10 percent for Asians.[24] In 1999, New York City police had an arrest rate following stops of 12.6 percent for whites, 11.5 percent for Latinos, and 10.5 percent for blacks.[25] If foreign or ethnic minority groups were committing more crime, they should be found to be breaking the law more often. In some contexts, the hit rate is actually lower for certain minority or foreign groups, suggesting lower offending rates. The data show that profiling immigrants and minorities is not productive.[26]

Reasons for stops: The effectiveness of police stops is strongly linked with the "grounds" or reason for which the stop was conducted. Across the European Union, police powers to conduct stops vary widely, from near total freedom to conduct identity checks, as in Hungary, to requiring that the officer have "reasonable suspicion" or an objective basis to think that a person has offended or is about to be involved in a crime, as in the United Kingdom.[27] When officers are required to record the reason for their suspicion, this information can be analyzed to see whether minority ethnic groups are being targeted for specific offenses, and whether the stops are in fact productive.

Discretion: The term discretion describes police officers' ability to decide when and when not to stop, check identity, search, and generally enforce the law. Police officers make the decision to stop and search people on the street, where they are often removed from direct supervision and thus have a great deal of discretion. However, these decisions are likely to be influenced by operational factors. It is possible to make a distinction between high- and low-discretion stops and searches.[28] High discretion stops and searches tend to be self-initiated activities by officers, whereas low-discretion stops refer to actions that have been directed by external factors, such as being called to an incident, information about an earlier incident providing suspect descriptions, and activity in relation to specific targeted operations.[29] Where levels of discretion are highest, officers' generalizations and stereotypes about likely offenders have greater scope for influencing decisions.[30]

In the United Kingdom, the 1984 Police and Criminal Evidence Act (PACE) governs police stops (except in alternative specific circumstances such as section 60 public order authority or section 44 counter-terror authority.[31]) Under PACE, police stops must be based on "reasonable suspicion" that the person has committed or is about to commit a crime. There is no similar requirement for section 60 stops, which were originally authorized for use at sporting events and similar circumstances, and which may be used over a limited time and in a defined area where there is the threat of serious violence or of people carrying weapons. Accordingly, officers enjoy more discretion when they conduct section 60 stops in the designated area.[32] Data for 2006–2007 show that under section 60, black people were 16.9 times more likely to be stopped and searched than white people, while Asian were 3.4 times more likely to be stopped and searched than whites when compared to their numbers within the residential population.[33] The number of arrests resulting from high-discretion stops is consistently lower.[34] Only 3.6 percent of stops and searches conducted pursuant to section 60 led to arrest in 2006–2007, significantly lower than the 12 percent arrest rate under the "reasonable suspicion" standard for stops.[35]

An examination of the grounds—the individualized factors that have led the officer to make the stop—recorded by officers[36] can determine whether searches meet the legal threshold of suspicion. In a 1999 study in New York City, the justification provided by officers for 15.4 percent of stops did not meet the legal standards and a quarter of the stop forms did not provide sufficient detail to determine if reasonable suspicion was present.[37] The absence of reasonable grounds can indicate that stop powers are being used for speculative "fishing expeditions" in the hope of discovering crime, or for other purposes such as asserting authority or maintaining order. Evidence that stops and searches without reasonable grounds are being used disproportionately against minority groups may indicate discrimination.

IV. STEPSS Data Analysis and Results

The stop data gathered by the STEPSS project clearly show that police in all three countries were engaged in ethnic profiling of minorities and immigrants. Minorities and immigrants were more likely to be stopped, often more likely to be searched, but, almost without exception, were no more likely to be found to be offending than the majority group. In some cases, they were significantly less likely to be found offending than majority residents. The data also demonstrate important benefits of monitoring stops in reducing levels of disproportionality and increasing the effectiveness of stops. During the project period, participating officers reduced the number of stops they made, but the proportion of stops that produced an arrest or other law enforcement outcome increased. This result is clearest in Fuenlabrada, but can also be seen in two pilot sites in Hungary, and is suggested by the Girona data. Further benefits can be seen in Fuenlabrada, where police managers and supervisors used the stop data to supervise individual officers more closely, and to examine the impact of specific operations and personnel deployments. The data enabled them to factor disproportionate ethnic impacts into their strategic decision-making and reduce unfair policing while enhancing efficiency.

Unfortunately, Bulgarian patrol officers failed to comply with STEPSS protocols and insufficient data were gathered to support a valid analysis. Nonetheless, the STEPSS experience in Bulgaria offers valuable lessons about the challenges inherent in measuring and addressing disproportionality. These challenges are explored further in the next chapter.

Fuenlabrada, Spain

During the six month pilot period of October 2007 through March 2008, the Fuenlabrada Municipal Police conducted 3,050 stops.[38] On an annual basis, this equates to 29 stops per 1,000 residents of Fuenlabrada.

Chart 1:
Fuenlabrada Municipal Police: Change in number of stops and searches over time
(October 2007–March 2008)

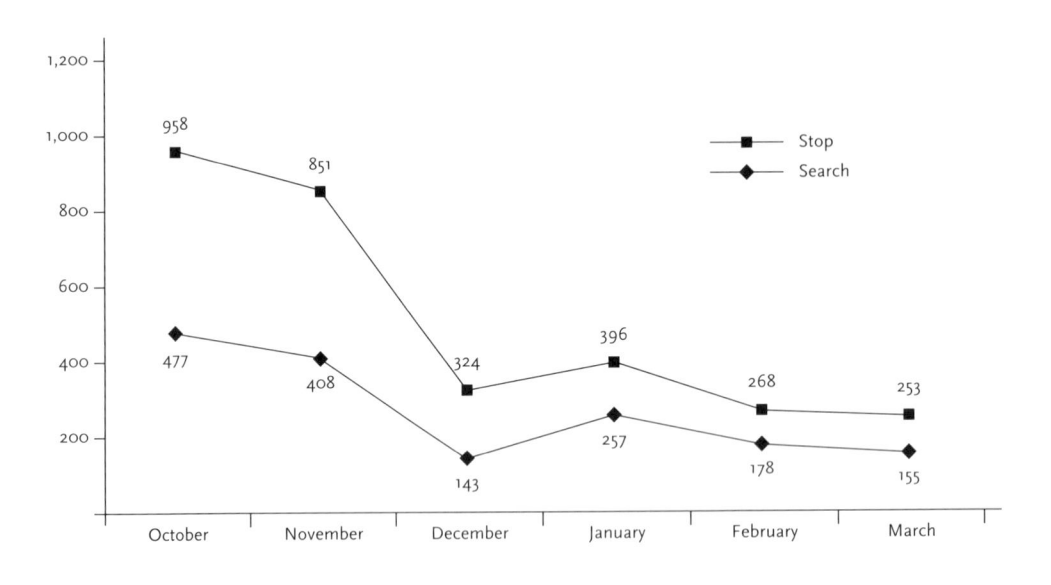

Month	Stop	Search
October	958	477
November	851	408
December	324	143
January	396	257
February	268	178
March	253	155

The number of recorded stops fell over the course of the project from 958 stops in October 2007 to 253 in March 2008. The number of searches conducted after stops also fell from 477 in October to 155 in March; and both stops and searches have continued at the lower level since the pilot program ended. While the rate of stops went down, their effectiveness increased.

Chart 2:

Fuenlabrada Municipal Police: Percentage of stops leading to positive results (Hit rate)

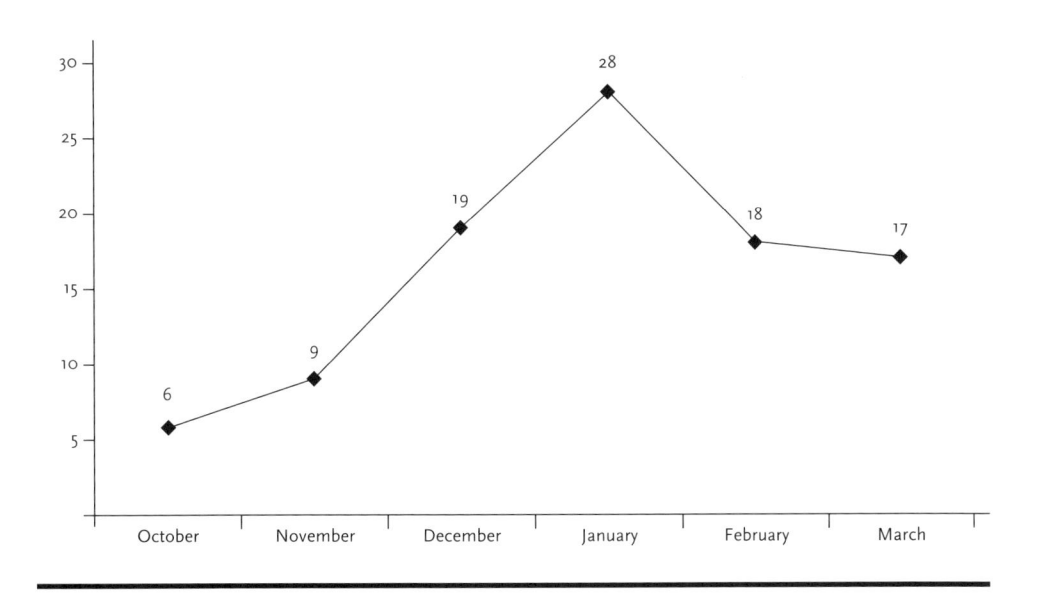

Month	Hit rate
October	6
November	9
December	19
January	28
February	18
March	17

The total number of positive outcomes—or hits—in Fuenlabrada was slightly lower for the project period compared to the six months preceding the project, reflecting the large drop in the number of stops made by officers.[39] However, the percentage of stops leading to positive results (or "hit rate") increased significantly as a result of the project. The improved hit rate suggests that the training and enhanced supervision implemented during the STEPSS project increased officer awareness of the criteria for using stops and improved their selection of people to stop. Stops were used more effectively and yielded better results while inconveniencing fewer people in the process.

Table 1 shows the relation of stops to searches for different ethnic groups in Fuenlabrada. Searches were conducted at roughly the same rate for all groups. But the hit rate varied significantly by group, from a hit rate of 17 percent for Spaniards, to a far lower seven percent rate for Moroccans, four percent for Romanians and Ecuadorians, two percent for Nigerians, and five percent for "others."[40] It is often argued that a disproportionate targeting of ethnic minority or immigrant groups is justified by differential rates of criminal involvement. The data here show that, in Fuenlabrada, minorities are far less likely to be found breaking the law than Spanish people and, consequently, it is not productive to stop and search the minority population a a higher rate.

Table 1:

Fuenlabrada Municipal Police: Stops, searches, and hit rates by nationality group

Ethnicity	Stops	Searches		Hit rate	
	Number	Number	Percentage of stops resulting in searches	Number	Percentage of stops resulting in a hit
Ecuadoran	139	74	53	5	4
Moroccan	319	166	52	23	7
Nigerian	133	46	35	2	2
Romanian	205	119	58	9	4
Spanish	1.886	1.028	55	327	17
Other	368	185	50	28	5
TOTAL	3.050	1.618	53	394	13

The aggregate data for the entire period show that minorities were in fact more likely to be stopped than ethnic Spaniards. The odds ratios show that Moroccans were 6.3 times more likely to be stopped than Spaniards, Romanians were 3.8 times more likely, Ecuadorians 3.9 times more likely, Nigerians 5.2 times more likely, and all other groups 2.1 times more likely to be stopped than Spanish people. The odds ratios are all greater than the 1.5 benign range and indicate that police are targeting immigrants.

Yet, there was an important reduction in levels of disproportionality during the project as shown in the chart below, which gives the odds ratio for each immigrant group by month. In the case of Moroccans the drop is particularly striking, from an odds ratio of 9.6 to one of 3.4. The drop in disproportionality reflects the willingness of Fuenlabrada's police to respond to community concerns and act upon the data. This is appropriate, because the hit rate data clearly showed that targeting minorities was not effective. The spike in stops of Nigerians in December reflects an anti-prostitution operation.

Chart 3:

Fuenlabrada Municipal Police: Disproportionality ratios over time (October 2007–March 2008)

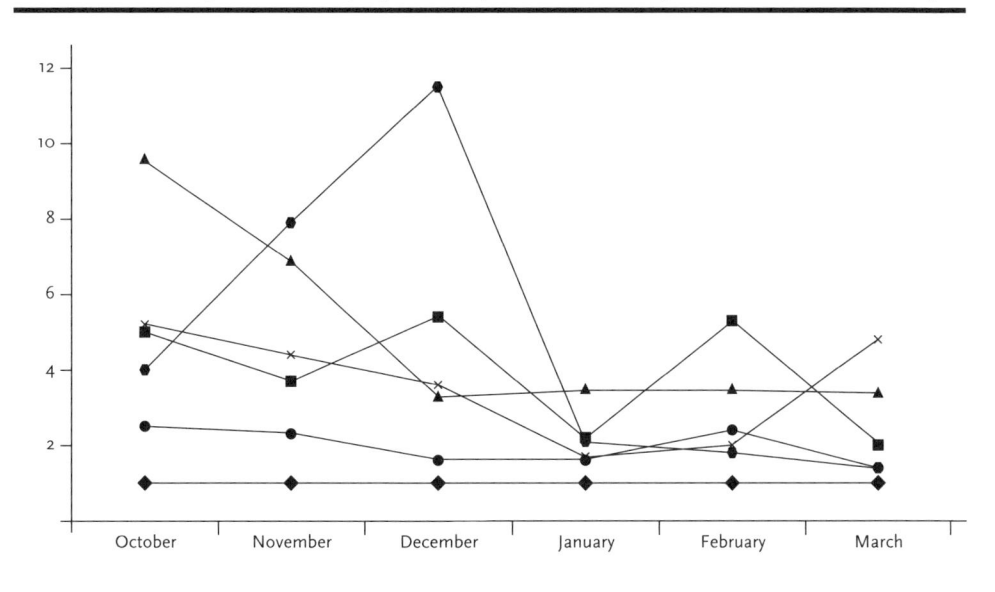

		October	November	December	January	February	March
◆	Spain	1.0	1.0	1.0	1.0	1.0	1.0
✕	Romania	5.2	4.4	3.6	1.7	2.0	4.8
▲	Morocco	9.6	6.9	3.3	3.5	3.5	3.4
■	Ecuador	5.0	3.7	5.4	2.2	5.3	2.0
●	Nigeria	4.0	7.9	11.5	2.1	1.8	1.4
●	Others	2.5	2.3	1.6	1.6	2.4	1.4

In addition to nationality, the STEPSS stop forms noted the type of operation under which the stop was conducted.[41] The majority of stops were conducted during operations focused on specific geographic areas or zones. A smaller number of stops were conducted on persons suspected of being wanted in relation to a previous offense or fitting a suspect description, or conducted as part of a preventive operation.

Type of Operation

Preventive operation: Operations designed to prevent crime and disorder. A counter-terrorism operation carried out during the project period fell into this category.

"Hot spot operation" or zone under intensive police control: Operations focused on specific areas or zones where intelligence indicates that certain crimes or infractions are being committed.

Identification of person wanted for administrative infraction or criminal offense: Stops conducted when it is believed that the person is wanted in relation to a previous offense or fits a suspect description.

Alleged uncivil conduct: Stops conducted in response to public disorder or perceived uncivil behavior, such as noisy drinking in public or playing loud music.

Suspicious attitude or behavior: Stops based on perceived suspicious behavior, nervousness, and evasive behavior.

Other: All other stops.

Chart 4:

Fuenlabrada Municipal Police: Stops by operation type or reason over time
(October 2007–March 2008)

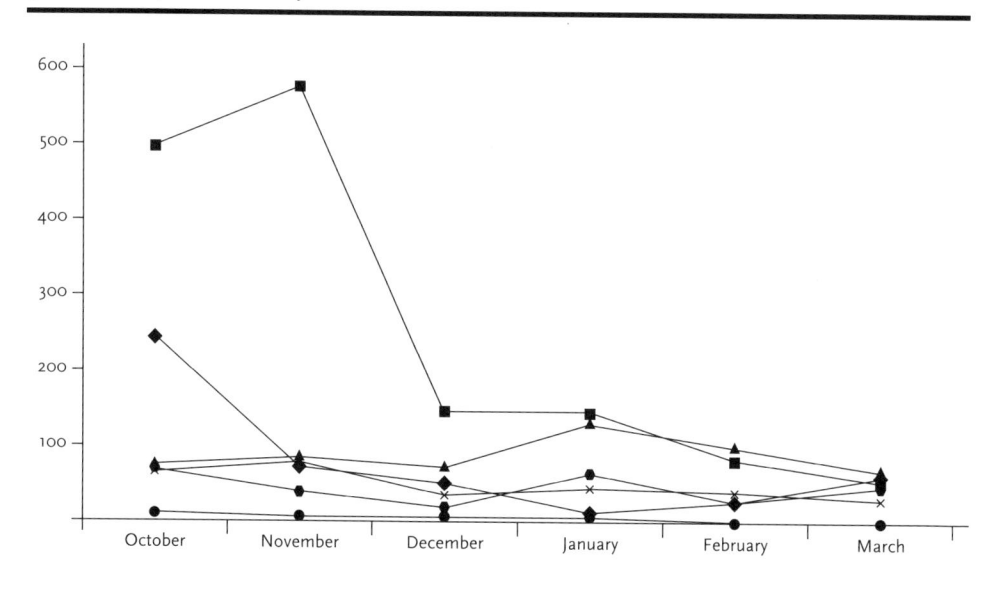

	October	November	December	January	February	March
♦ Preventive operation	243	71	50	11	25	59
■ Zone under intensive police control	496	575	145	143	80	52
▲ Wanted person for criminal or administrative offense	75	86	73	131	100	69
● Alleged participation in uncivil conduct	70	38	18	63	25	45
× Suspicious behavior or conduct	64	76	34	43	38	28
● Others	10	5	4	5	0	0

The drop in stop rates during the project is primarily due to reduced use of three types of police operations: zones under intensive police control (also called "hot spot operations"), preventive operations, and stops for suspicious attitude or behavior. Stops under these categories fell by 90 percent, 76 percent and 56 percent respectively during the project period.

During preventive and hot spot operations, officers are provided with guidelines on whom to stop, based on either the type of crime they are trying to prevent (such as a terrorist attack) or on intelligence that particular crimes are happening in specific areas. The project data suggest that in these types of operations patrol officers were more aggressive and used more speculative reasoning and stereotypes in deciding whom to stop. This may be because the officers themselves did not have to articulate the reason for a stop during these operations—the nature of the operation itself provided a reason.

Conversely, officers used stops more carefully and efficiently when they were required to justify the stops. The hit rates support this conclusion. Hit rates were higher for the three types of stops that require officers to be able to articulate grounds for stopping someone: a 33 percent hit rate for identifying the perpetrator of a crime or administrative infraction; a 10 percent hit rate for alleged uncivil conduct; and a 15 percent hit rate for suspicious behavior. All of these are significantly higher than the three percent hit rate for preventive operations and the nine percent rate for hot spot operations.[42]

The numbers of stops ascribed to "suspicious behavior" dropped by 56 percent during the STEPSS project. Suspicious behavior stops are high discretion stops based on an officer's subjective assessment of behavior. Suspicious behavior stops accounted for nine percent of all stops of Spanish people, but 16 percent of all stops of Moroccan people and 12 percent of all stops of Romanians. The reduction of suspicious behavior stops during the project made an important contribution to the overall drop in disproportionality for Moroccans and Romanians.

It is useful to look at stop patterns of the two largest immigrant groups in Fuenlabrada, Romanians and Moroccans, as they demonstrate the disproportionate impacts that certain operations have on specific groups.

Chart 5:

Fuenlabrada Municipal Police: Change over time in stops of Romanians (October 2007–March 2008)

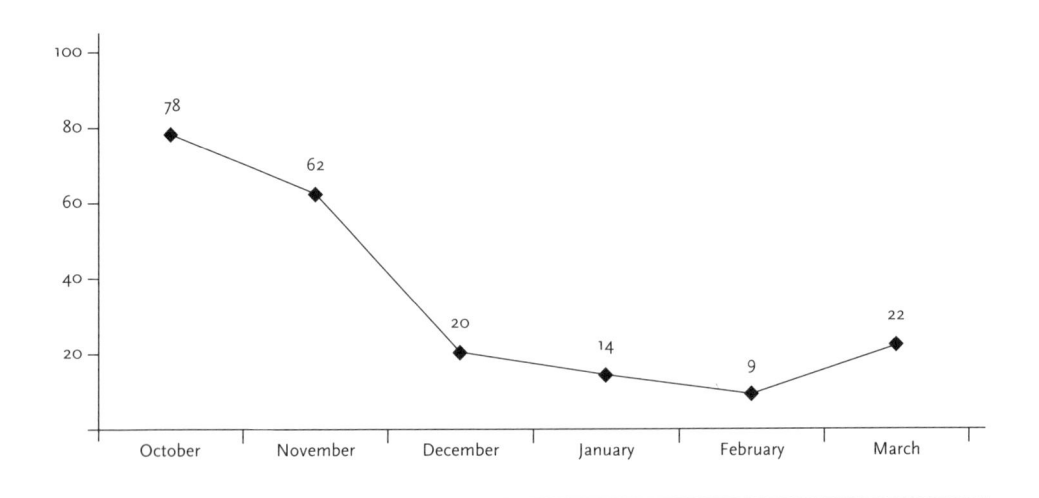

Month	Stops
October	78
November	62
December	20
January	14
February	9
March	22

In October and November, large numbers of Romanian women were stopped (78 and 62 respectively for each month; with odds ratios of 5.2 and 4.4). The vast majority of these stops (77 and 69 percent respectively) were conducted under hot spot operations targeting prostitution in one area. At the community consultation meetings, the police explained that they had received complaints about prostitution in that area and the operation was aimed at displacing prostitutes through the aggressive use of stops and outreach to prostitution support groups.[43] The operation ended in December when the women moved out of the area, and the numbers of stops on Romanians fell dramatically and were no longer concentrated under hot stop operations.[44]

Chart 6:

Fuenlabrada Municipal Police: Change over time in stops of Moroccans (October 2007–March 2008)

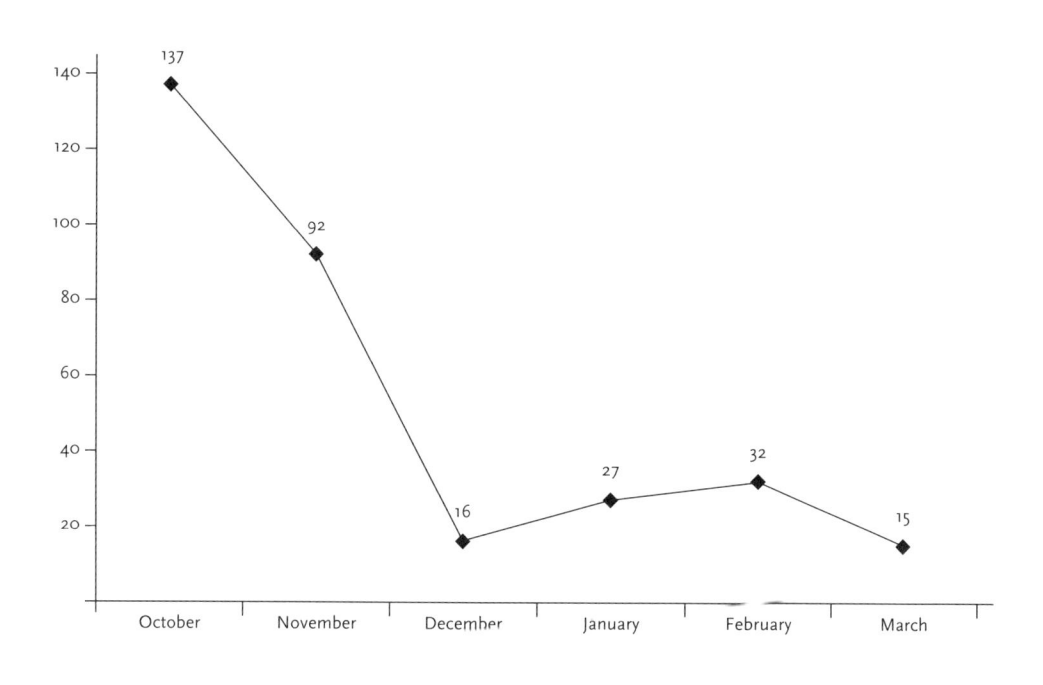

Month	Stops
October	137
November	92
December	16
January	27
February	32
March	15

The pattern of stops on Moroccans throughout the project period is also illustrative. The first two months of stop data showed high levels of stops of Moroccans—especially young Moroccan men—under preventive operations, hot spots, and suspicious behavior categories (28 percent, 37 percent and 16 percent respectively). As the numbers of stops conducted under these three operations fell dramatically, so did the level of disproportionality in stops of Moroccans. For example, stops of Moroccans under preventive operations fell by 97 percent over the course of the project. In October, there were 137 stops of Moroccans; that is 14 percent of all stops that month despite the fact that Moroccans represent only 2.2 percent of the residential population (an odds ratio of 9.6). Sixty-five of those 137 stops took place under a preventive operation conducted for counter-terrorism.[45] As only one stop in October (and none in November) had a positive result, there was no clear operational impact in terms of law enforcement, but discussions in the monthly community meetings made clear the negative impact in the Moroccan community. In late November the police cancelled the operation. Since December, stops of Moroccans remained relatively steady, rising slightly in February, which the police explained was in response to an anti-drug dealing operation based on time-bound and area specific intelligence (a hot spot operation).

Girona, Spain[46]

In reviewing data from Girona, it is necessary to account for two police forces working the same area with different legal mandates, and different policing styles and levels of reliance on stops. The Girona Municipal Police are responsible for community policing, petty crime, and civic and administrative infractions, while the Mossos d'Esquadra regional police have responsibility for more serious crimes, and rely less on stops in their investigations. Also it is important to note that the Mossos d'Esquadra had special units operating in Girona that did not participate in the STEPSS project and were not recording their actions; this limits the conclusions that can be drawn from the data. During the six-month project period (which was the same in Girona and Fuenlabrada—October 2007 to March 2008), the municipal police recorded 1,526 stops, and the Mossos d'Esquadra recorded 902 stops.[47] This equates to 32 stops per 1,000 residents for the municipal police, and 19 recorded stops per 1,000 residents for the Mossos d'Esquadra. Both forces make most stops at night, and primarily stop young men, but beyond these simple parallels their stop patterns vary considerably.

The number of stops made by the municipal police dropped in November and then continued at a steady level for the rest of the project period; searches also fell significantly in November, but then continued to decline more gradually for the rest of the project.

Chart 7:

Girona Municipal Police: Change over time in stops and searches (October 2007–March 2008)

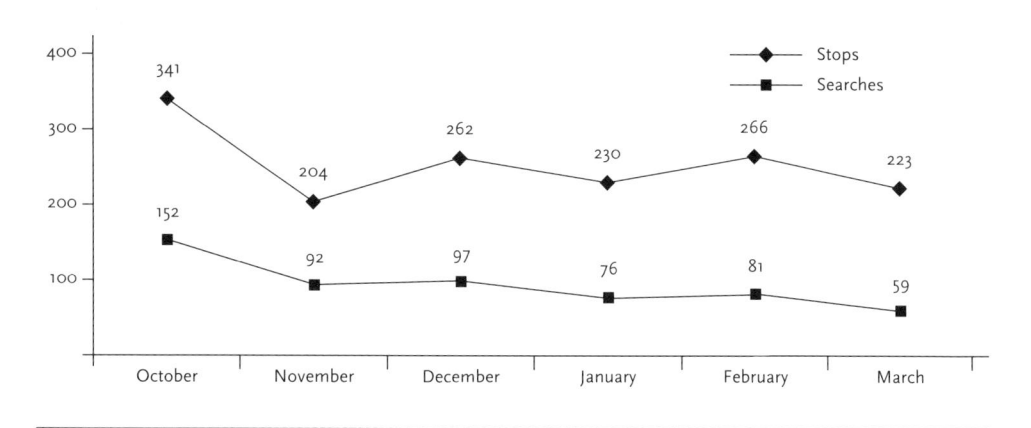

	October	November	December	January	February	March
Stops	341	204	262	230	266	223
Searches	152	92	97	76	81	59

The Mossos stop and search pattern is a little different, and shows a clear drop through the first part of the project period, followed by a return to previous levels. Several explanations are possible: this may reflect initial compliance with the STEPSS protocols followed by a loss of interest and reduction in recording stops, with a return to recording just before the end of the project; or it may reflect a temporary reaction against the stop forms as manifested by police carrying out fewer stops (called a "dampening effect" or "de-policing") with stops returning to former levels once officers became accustomed to completing the forms

Chart 8:

Girona Mossos d'Esquadra: Change over time in stops and searches (October 2007–March 2008)

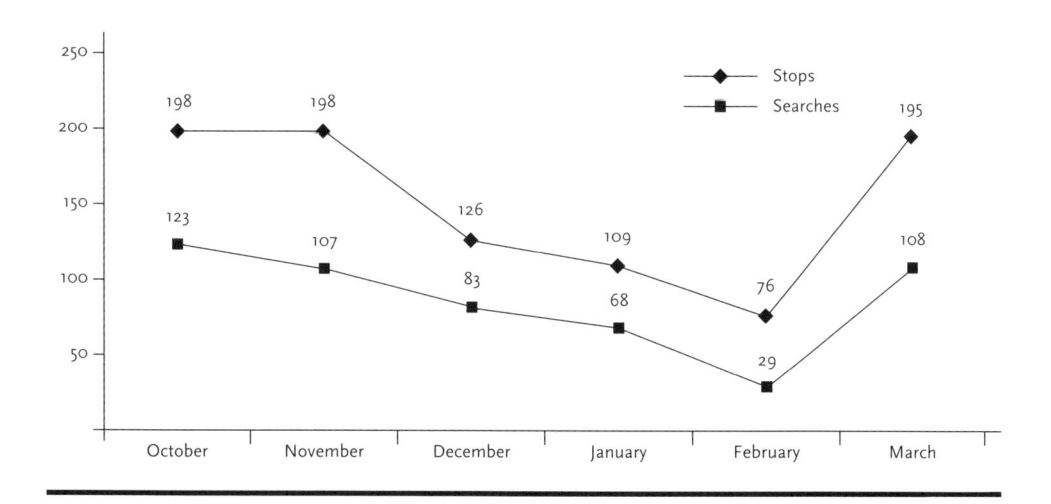

	October	November	December	January	February	March
Stops	198	198	126	109	76	195
Searches	123	107	83	68	29	108

In contrast to their varying stop and search rates, the hit rate pattern for each force is similar.[48] The percentage of stops leading to a hit drops off significantly and then rises somewhat toward the end of the project period. For the Mossos d'Esquadra, this echoes the fall and rebound in the overall number of stops and searches, but it is unclear why the drop occurred for the municipal police.

Chart 9:
Girona Municipal Police: Percentage of stops leading to positive results (Hit rate)
(October 2007–March 2008)

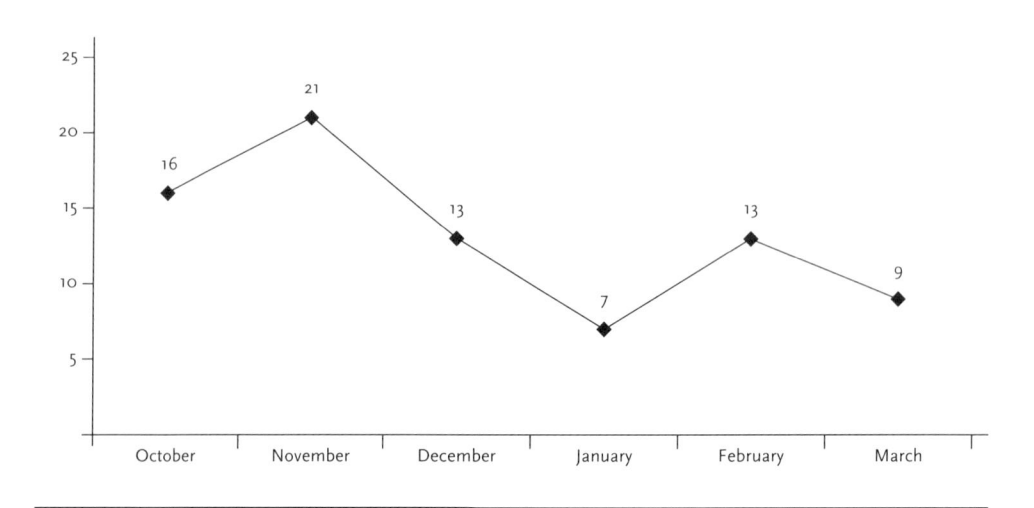

Month	Hit rate
October	16
November	21
December	13
January	7
February	13
March	9

Chart 10:
Girona Mossos d'Esquadra: Percentage of stops leading to positive results (Hit rate)
(October 2007–March 2008)

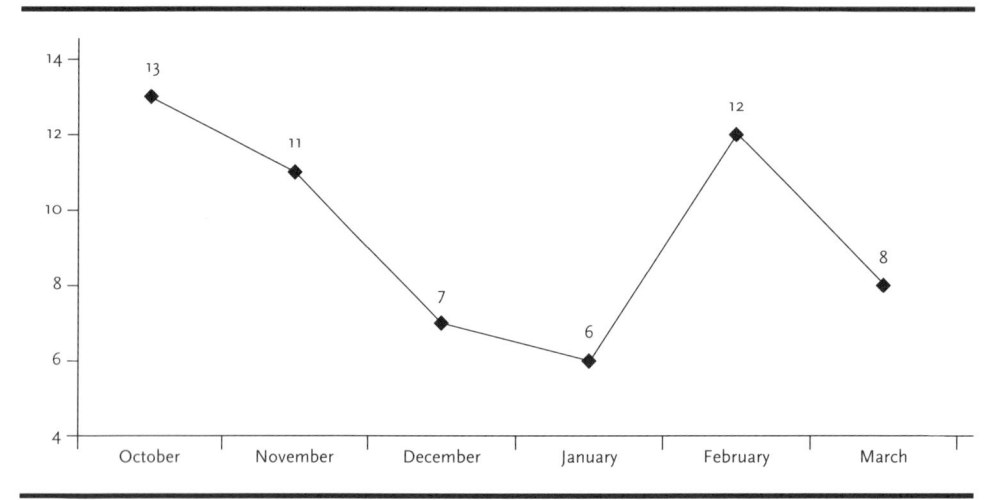

Month	Hit rate
October	13
November	11
December	7
January	6
February	12
March	8

The Girona data do not show strong or consistent enough trends to draw firm conclusions. But it is worth noting that there is a clear correlation between a low number of recorded stops and higher hit rates, as can be seen in the November numbers for the municipal police and the February data for the Mossos in the above charts.

Table 2:

Girona Municipal Police: Odds ratios(October 2007–March 2008)[49]

Nationality	Stops	Resident population	Stops per 1,000 residents	Odds ratio
Honduran	920	2,557	35.9	3.9
Moroccan	244	3,930	62.0	6.7
Romanian	144	1,560	92.3	10.0
Spanish	707	76,483	9.2	1.0
Others	339	11,931	28.4	3.0

Foreigners are disproportionately targeted for stops by both police forces in Girona. The Mossos d'Equadra odds ratios were especially high: Moroccans were 6.7 times more likely to be stopped than a Spanish person, and Romanians 10 times more likely. The large number of youths in the immigrant population, and lifestyles involving greater presence on the street than Spaniards, means that these groups are more available to be stopped. Yet the disproportionality ratios are so high that even accounting for these factors, these groups are clearly being profiled by the police.

Table 3:

Girona Mossos d'Esquadra: Odds ratios (October 2007–March 2008)

Nationality	Stops	Resident population	Stops per 1,000 residents	Odds ratio
Honduran	30	2,557	11.7	2.1
Moroccan	213	3,930	54.1	10.0
Romanian	52	1,560	33.3	6.1
Spainish	415	76,483	5.4	1.0
Other	192	11,931	16.0	2.9

The data show that the Mossos d'Esquadra also disproportionally target their stops on certain foreign groups: Moroccans are 10 times more likely to be stopped than Spanish people, Romanians are 6.1 times more likely to be stopped; Hondurans are 2.1 times more likely to be stopped and all other groups are 2.9 times more likely to be stopped than Spanish people. These figures indicate ethnic profiling.

Chart 11:

Girona Municipal Police: Diproportionality over time (October 2007–March 2008)

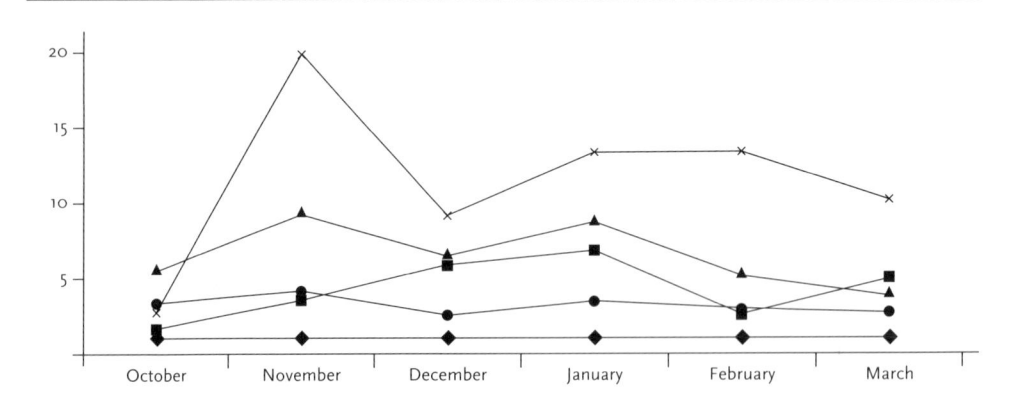

	October	November	December	January	February	March
Spain	1.0	1.0	1.0	1.0	1.0	1.0
Romania	2.7	19.8	9.1	13.3	13.5	10.3
Morocco	5.6	9.4	6.6	8.8	5.3	4.0
Honduras	1.6	3.5	5.8	6.8	2.5	5.0
Others	3.3	4.1	2.5	3.4	2.9	2.7

Charts 11 and 12 represent disproportionality ratios in both forces over the course of the project period. Disproportionality within the municipal police remained steady throughout: it rose slightly and then fell for Romanians but stayed at around the same rates for all other groups. Interestingly, the data for the Mossos d'Esquadra show that disproportionality actually rose during the project period and then fell to levels similar to those at the project's beginning. Given the additional scrutiny that police officers were under during the project, it is surprising that they targeted foreigners in higher numbers during this time. It is possible that the rise in disproportionality reflects resistance to the project. Officers complained that the project was questioning their professionalism and in effect calling them racists. Another explanation is that the data were not being analyzed and fed back to the police force in a regular manner, and therefore did not inform police practice—and perhaps prompt change—as they did in Fuenlabrada.

Chart 12:

Girona Mossos d'Esquadra: Diproportionality over time (October 2007–March 2008)

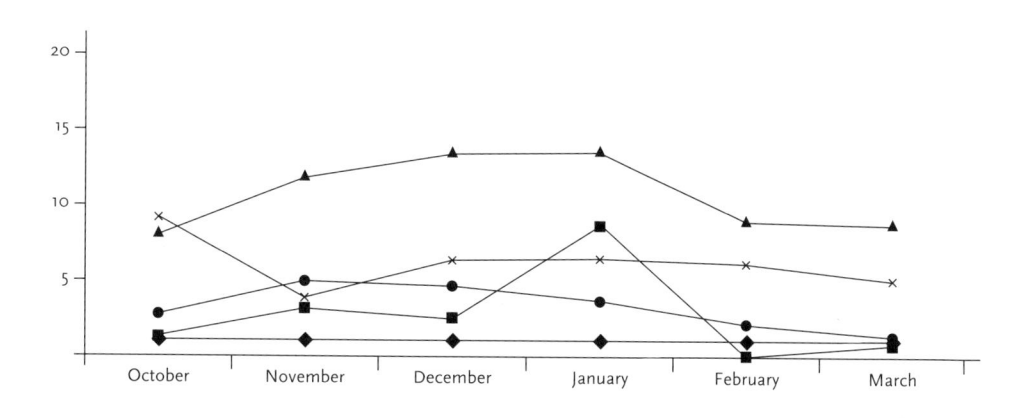

	October	November	December	January	February	March
Spain	1.0	1.0	1.0	1.0	1.0	1.0
Romania	9.1	3.8	6.3	6.4	6.1	5.0
Morocco	8.1	11.9	13.5	13.6	9.0	8.8
Honduras	1.2	3.1	2.5	8.6	0.0	0.7
Others	2.7	4.9	4.6	3.6	2.1	1.3

Table 4:
Girona Mossos d'Esquadra: Stops, searches and hit rates by nationality group

Nationality	Stops Number	Searches Number	Percentage of stops resulting in searches	Hit rate Number	Percentage of stops resulting in a hits
Honduran	30	10	33	0	0
Moroccan	213	150	70	24	11
Romanian	52	40	77	9	17
Spanish	415	215	52	38	9
Others	192	103	54	14	7
TOTAL	902	518	57	85	9

What transpires immediately after a stop is equally important in detecting discrimination and exploring issues of police effectiveness. The Girona data show that the municipal police searched an average of 37 percent of those they stopped, with a slightly higher rate for Romanians. In contrast, the Mossos d'Esquadra searched an average of 57 percent of those they stopped. Although some minority groups were searched at lower rates, Moroccans and Romanians were searched by the Mossos d'Esquadra 70 and 77 percent of the times that they are stopped, respectively. These numbers show that police officers are acting on the assumption that they are more likely to find illegal goods or weapons on immigrants. Yet the data show that this perception is wrong. Overall, the municipal police got positive results from 13 percent of their stops while the Mossos d'Esquadra got positive results from just nine percent of their stops. Most immigrant groups are no more likely than Spaniards to be found breaking the law. (Romanians were the exception.)[50] The data clearly demonstrate that it is not productive to stop and search immigrants at greater rates than Spanish people in Girona.

"MOROCCANS CARRY KNIVES"

Both police forces in Girona stop a highly disproportionate number of Moroccans and the hit rate for these stops is very low. Representatives of both police forces explained that this reflects self-protection measures taken by police officers who believe that Moroccans habitually carry knives. Data on hit rates show that in fact other nationalities, and Spaniards in particular, are more likely to carry weapons. The data clearly show that this "common knowledge" about Moroccans is a pejorative stereotype.

Data gathered during the project period allow an analysis of the number of stops, searches, and positive results that were conducted under directed and non-directed operations.[51]

Under directed operations, officers are told by commanding officers whom they should stop based on the type of crime the operation is meant to prevent or on the basis of intelligence about particular crimes in particular areas. Because directed operations are ordered by senior officers, the police on the street who are carrying out the operation do not have to justify their stops and thus have more leeway to indulge in stereotyping and generalizations. For this reason, directed operations are generally less effective than stops that individual officers have to justify to their commanders as based on well-grounded suspicion. This highlights the need to improve the intelligence on which directed operations are based and provide better guidelines to officers on who to stop during such operations. It would also help if officers were required to justify their stops even during directed operations.

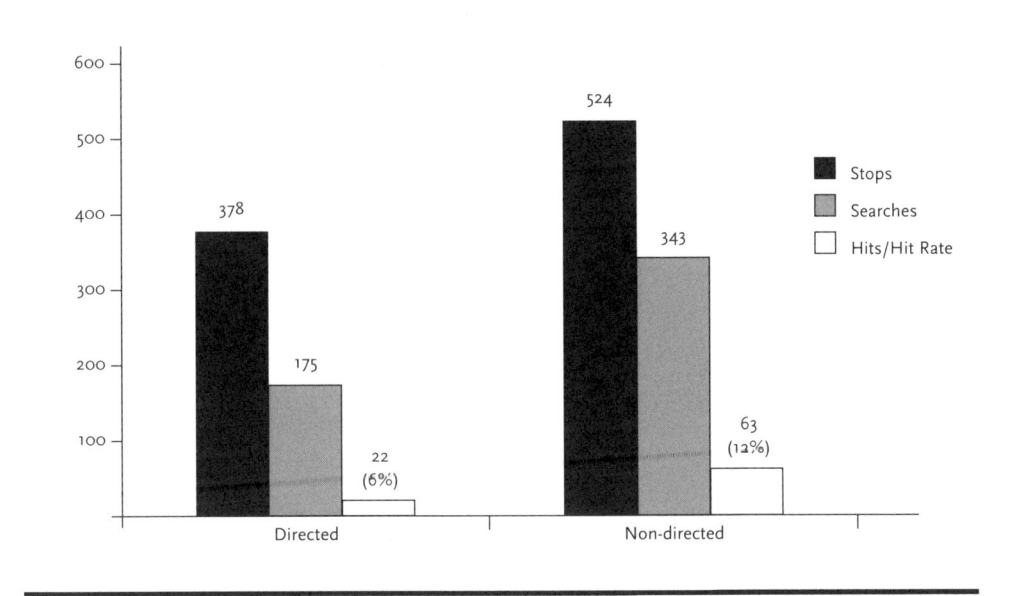

Chart 13:

Girona Municipal Police: Type of operation and results (October 2007–March 2008)

Operation	Stops	Searches	Hits/Hit Rate
Directed	378	175	22 (6%)
Non-directed	524	343	63 (12%)

Chart 14:

Girona Mossos d'Esquadra: Type of operation and results (October 2007–March 2008)

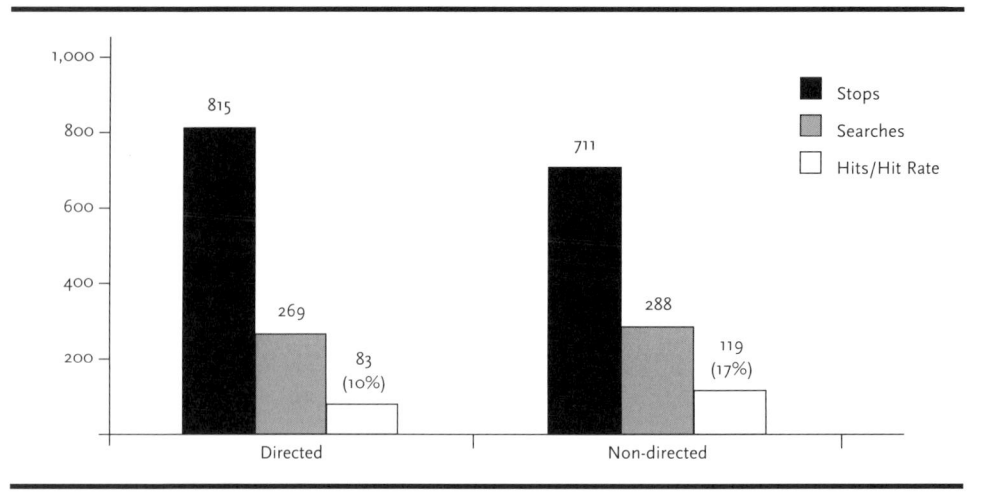

[Bar chart showing:
- Directed: Stops 815, Searches 269, Hits 83 (10%)
- Non-directed: Stops 711, Searches 288, Hits 119 (17%)]

Fifty-four percent of the municipal police stops were part of directed operations, whereas 42 percent of stops conducted by the Mossos d'Esquadra were part of directed operations. As in Fuenlabrada, stops conducted under directed operations are much less productive. Directed stops conducted by the municipal police had a hit rate of 10 percent, compared to 17 percent for non-directed stops; for the Mossos d'Esquadra the hit rate for directed stops was six percent compared to 12 percent for non-directed stops.

Hungary

In Hungary, stop data were gathered between September 17, 2007 and March 17, 2008. Over this period, the police in the three pilot sites carried out 35,954 stops;[52] of these, 22,375 were recorded on the STEPSS forms.

Table 5:

Hungary: Total stops recorded by the police compared to stops recorded on STEPSS forms

Location	Number of stops	Percentage of total	Number of STEPSS forms completed	Percentage of total	STEPSS forms completed compared to total number of stops (percentage)
Budapest	3,033	8	2,015	8	66
Kaposvár	22,089	61	13,506	55	61
Szeged	10,832	31	9,105	37	84
TOTAL	35,954	100	24,626	100	68

Table 6:

Hungary: Stops per 1,000 population

Location	Number of stops	Estimated population	Number of stops per 1,000 population per year
Budapest[53]	6,065	65,000	65 stops per 1,000
Kaposvár[54]	44,177	122,000	325 stops per 1,000
Szeged[55]	23,633	203,000	93 stops per 1,000

The table above illustrates the number of people stopped per 1,000 of the estimated local population. The numbers of stops conducted in the three pilot sites are staggeringly high. Hungarian law gives police much greater latitude for making stops than police in other EU countries enjoy. As a result, Hungarian police have contact with the general public through stops at much higher rates than police in other European countries.

Chart 15:

Hungary: Number of stops (September 2007–March 2008)

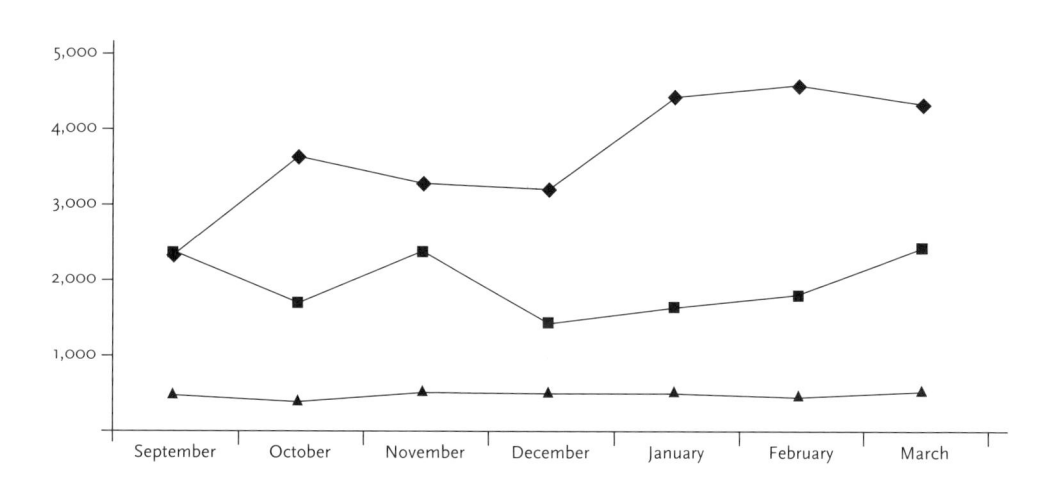

	September	October	November	December	January	February	March
Kaposvár	2,327	3,631	3,282	3,204	4,429	4,573	4,324
Szeged	2,368	1,704	2,380	1,445	1,650	1,805	2,434
Budapest (6th District)	498	411	540	525	533	483	548

The number of stops recorded in Hungary during the project period varied considerably among the three cities, as seen in the table above. There were particularly conspicuous differences between Szeged and Kaposvár, with very high stop levels in the latter despite a substantially smaller population. The differences reflect recording practices and different policing styles. Following guidelines given by the county headquarters, the Kaposvár Police place greater emphasis on the use of stops for "screening and mapping." This use of stops is questionable in light of the data on effectiveness.

In Hungary, the police define a successful stop (or "hit") as one that yields any of the three following positive outcomes: (a) arrests; (b) short-term arrests;[56] and (c) petty offense procedures initiated. Petty offenses are quasi-criminal offenses, the gravity of which does not reach the criminal level.[57]

The aggregate data from all three sites over the six month project period—including traffic stops[58]—show that only one percent of stops led to arrest, two percent led to short term arrest, and 18 percent led to petty offense procedures being instigated. These are very low hit rates, indicating that large numbers of people were inconvenienced by police stops with little result. These data call into question the argument that extensive checks are an effective crime fighting tool and point to a great deal of time wasted by police conducting fruitless stops.

Chart 16:

Hungary: Grounds for stops (including traffic stops)

Grounds	Percent
Posession of legally prohibited object	0.1
Suspicious object	0.2
Prevention of an act jeopardizing public order	0.3
Security measure	0.4
Finding a wanted person	0.5
Suspicion of crime	2
Intensive control	8
Suspicion of petty offense	19
Other	33
Traffic control	38

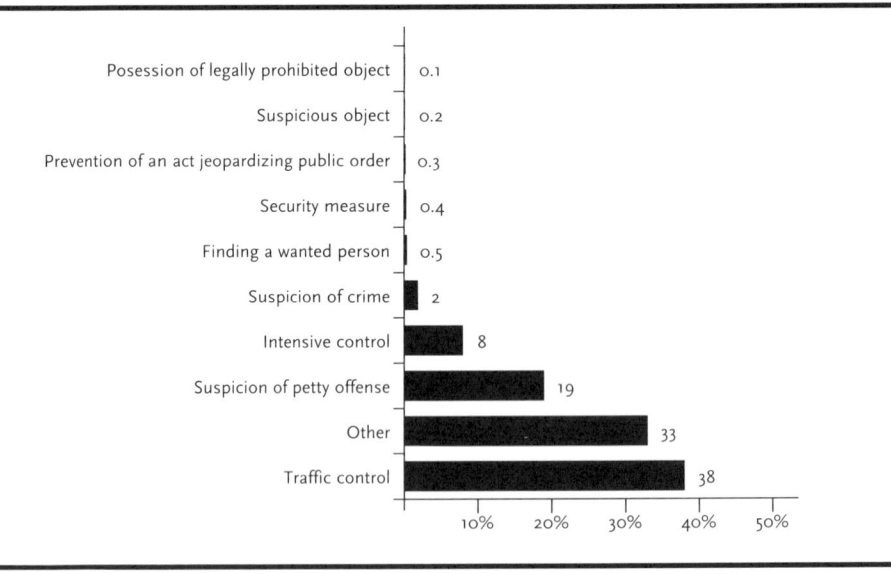

Of the stops recorded in Hungary during the project period, 37 percent were traffic stops. A relatively high proportion of stops, 19 percent, were petty offense stops; eight percent were conducted for intensive controls; and only two percent of stops were related to the suspicion of a criminal act. A third of the stops were recorded under the "other" category; and this rises to 50 percent when traffic stops are removed from the data.

Traffic stops and intensive control stops are often performed as part of large-scale operations, based on an order from a superior, with the objective of arresting a criminal suspect or preventing crime or violence. In these operations, all persons entering a specific area are stopped and their identity documents checked. Traffic stops—the most common type of stop—accounted for only 16 percent of the petty offense procedures initiated. The negligible hit rates for these types of stops indicate they were based on inadequate intelligence or insufficient instruction being given to officers, resulting in large numbers of people being stopped with little result.

In half the traffic stops and a third of pedestrian stops, the grounds for the stop—as marked on the officer's stop form—were given as "other." Where officers checked the "other" box, the stop forms contained an open field for them to record the reasons for the stop. Many officers were unable to articulate any concrete grounds for stops listed as "other." In 64 percent of these cases officers entered no information in the open field, and in 20 percent the information provided was unsatisfactory (for example, officers frequently indicated "general identity check" as the reason).[59] Although the threshold for conducting stops in Hungary is extremely low, stops conducted for no reason or insufficient reason violate the Hungarian Police Act, which requires that stops have a specific purpose. When officers cannot articulate the reason for a stop, that stop is unlikely to produce a positive result.

CHANGES IN NUMBERS OF STOPS AND EFFECTIVENESS IN BUDAPEST AND SZEGED

In the Sixth District of Budapest there was a dramatic, 75.3 percent, decrease in stops (from 14,362 to 3,538) during the project period, as compared to the same period in the previous year. The decline in the number of stops was accompanied by an increase in overall effectiveness. Over the course of data gathering, 2,242 petty offense proceedings were initiated compared to 977 such measures in the same period of the previous year—a 129 percent increase. The number of short-term arrests remained stable (692 persons taken into custody compared to 683 in the same period of the preceding year). There was a ten percent drop in the identification of persons wanted on an arrest warrant (which mirrors similar drops in this category nationwide).

Chart 17:

Budapest, Hungary: Number of stops in September 2007–March 2008 compared to the number of stops in September 2006–March 2007

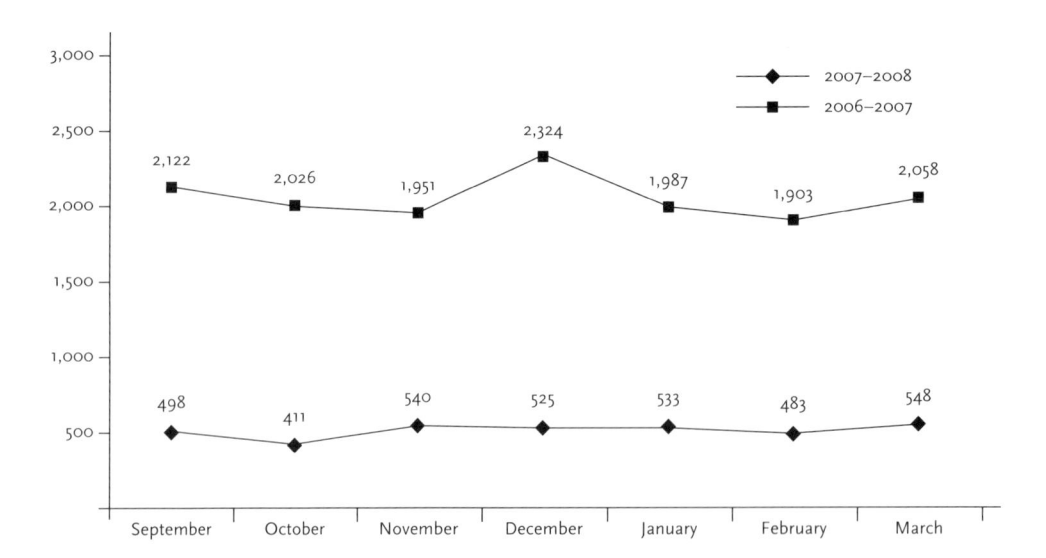

```
3,000
                                                                    ◆  2007–2008
                                                                    ■  2006–2007
2,500
                              2,324
       2,122
              2,026                        1,987              2,058
2,000         1,951                              1,903


1,500


1,000
        498         540    525    533         548
              411                       483
 500


       September  October  November  December  January  February  March
```

Supervisors explained that this sharp drop in the number of stops in the Sixth District could result from briefings that ordered officers to refrain from stopping a person unless they had concrete and identifiable grounds. Furthermore, officers faced the administrative burden of filling out the STEPSS form in addition to their regular forms. As one supervisor noted in the project evaluation interviews:

> Prior to the project, officers might have selected people randomly, but after the project started, officers knew that they had to have a firm reason for stopping people. It was explained in the briefing that the firm reason couldn't be color of skin or clothes—so this could be the reason why the number of stops dropped dramatically.

In his view, because officers had to consider the grounds for their stops, they focused more on checking suspected perpetrators of petty and criminal offenses reflected in the increase in those categories. The decrease in arrests of persons found to have outstanding arrest warrants was explained by the overall number of stops carried out. In the six months following the end of STEPSS, the number of stops increased by 25 percent in the Sixth District.

Chart 18:

Szeged, Hungary: Number of stops in September 2007–March 2008 compared to the number of stops in September 2006–March 2007

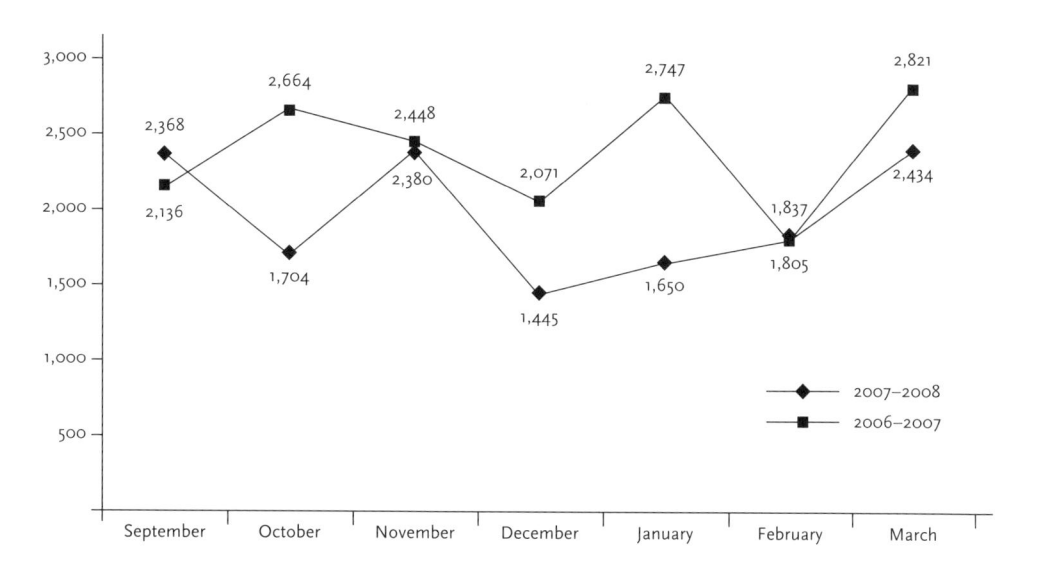

In Szeged, the total overall number of stops dropped by 17.5 percent (from 16,724 to 13,786) compared to the same period of the previous year. At the same time, overall efficiency seems to have increased. Although fewer petty offense proceedings were initiated (3,036 instead of 3,361) and fewer on-the-spot fines were imposed (2,718 as opposed to 3,630), the number of short-term arrests and the number of persons with a pending arrest warrant who were identified and arrested increased slightly (from 605 to 611 and from 148 to 163 respectively). Senior officers explained that this increase was achieved by creating a specialized search unit whose sole purpose is finding and arresting wanted persons. The unit is using stops and identity checks not as a general screening method, but only on a targeted basis.

The decrease in the number of stops in Budapest's Sixth District and Szeged was accompanied by an increase in the overall effectiveness of stops in these two pilot sites. The increased scrutiny of stops introduced as a result of the project led to a reduction in the numbers of stops. When officers focus on individualized suspicion rather than preconceptions about particular ethnic groups, they are more effective. The experience in Szeged also shows that targeted operations that do not rely on stops are more effective than the use of traffic or preventive operations that rely on stopping everyone. Results show that reducing stops through tightened supervision can lead to increased effectiveness while inconveniencing far fewer people in the process.

Chart 19:

Hungary: Officer perception of people stopped (September 2007–March 2008)

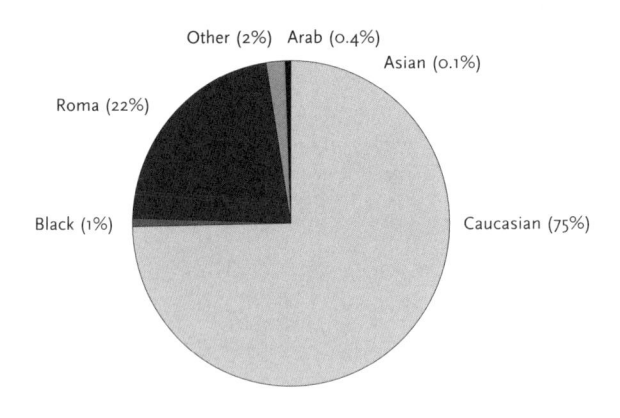

- Other (2%)
- Arab (0.4%)
- Asian (0.1%)
- Roma (22%)
- Black (1%)
- Caucasian (75%)

The data from Hungary show that Roma were disproportionately targeted for stops; 22 percent of all persons stopped by police were Roma[60] while 75 percent were identified as Caucasian. The remaining three percent were identified as black, Arab, Asian, or other. Population estimates vary but the most reliable put the Roma population of Hungary at about 620,000 of the population of 10,045,000, or 6.2 percent.[61] Roma youth were especially likely to be targeted for stops: Roma youth ages 15 through 19 make up 10.3 percent of the Roma population but accounted for 32 percent of all Roma who were stopped.[62]

The disproportionality with which Roma were targeted for stops varied considerably among the three pilot sites, as seen in the bar graph below.[63]

Chart 20:

Hungary: Percentage of stops on those perceived to be Roma compared to their estimate percentage of the population (September 2007–March 2008)

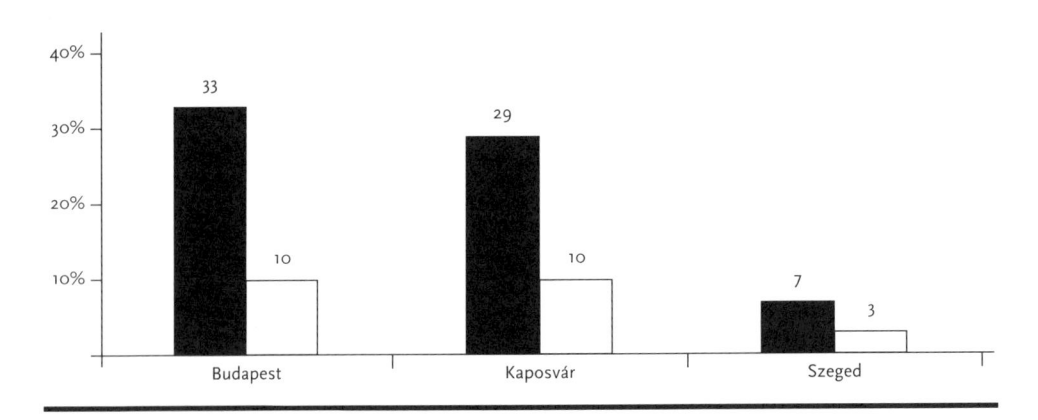

Site	Stops (%)	Population (%)
Budapest	33	10
Kaposvár	29	10
Szeged	7	3

The odds ratios for each area are: 3.3 for Roma in Budapest; 3 for Szeged; and 2 for Kaposvár (rising to 2.4 when traffic stops are excluded from the data set).

The data also show considerable differences in the grounds under which ethnic groups are stopped. Roma are over-represented in almost every category. The disproportionality is particularly acute for high-discretion stops where negative stereotypes come into play, such as suspicion of petty offense or crime, possession of a legally prohibited item, possession of a suspicious object, prevention of an act jeopardizing public order, and "other." In all of these scenarios, Roma are stopped disproportionately.

Chart 21:

Hungary: Grounds for stops by ethnicity (September 2007–March 2008)

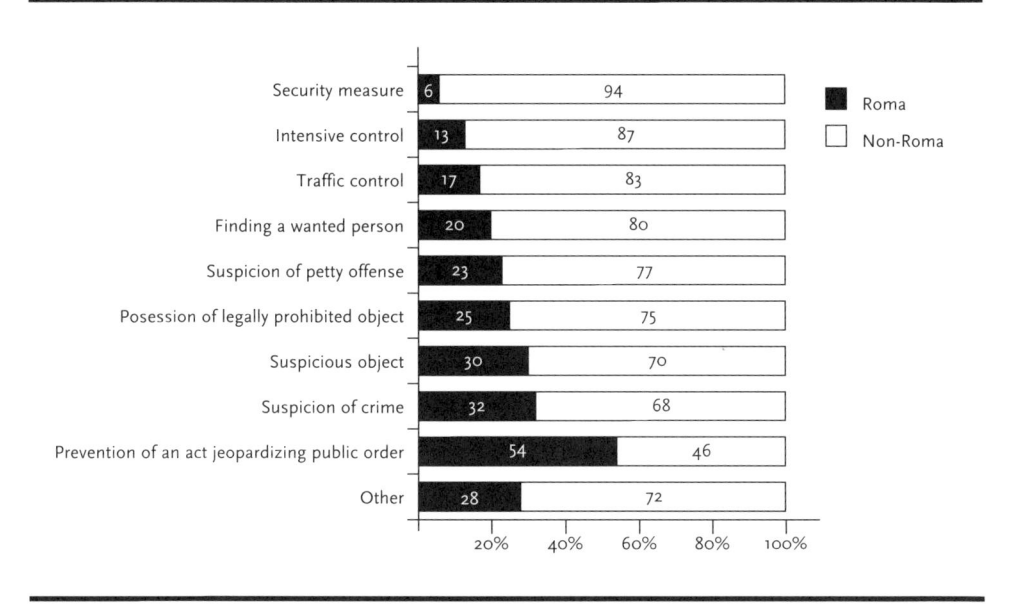

Grounds	Roma	Non-Roma
Security measure	6	94
Intensive control	13	87
Traffic control	17	83
Finding a wanted person	20	80
Suspicion of petty offense	23	77
Posession of legally prohibited object	25	75
Suspicious object	30	70
Suspicion of crime	32	68
Prevention of an act jeopardizing public order	54	46
Other	28	72

Although Roma are stopped disproportionately, the hit rate is the same for Roma and non-Roma. At the national level, 78 percent of stops of Roma and 79 percent of stops of non-Roma produced no result—a virtually identical rate. Similarly, the percentage of stops followed by a petty offense proceeding for Roma and non-Roma was 19 and 18 percent respectively. Rates of arrests and short term arrests are practically the same for the Roma and non-Roma samples. It is often argued that Roma are targeted because they have a higher rate of offending. The data do not support this assertion; the stop data find both Roma and non-Roma offending at very similar rates.

When the data are differentiated by pilot site, a significant difference in hit rates emerges. In Budapest, 41 percent of stops of non-Roma, produced a positive result, but only 20 percent of stops of Roma did so. However, 33 percent of all the persons stopped were Roma, even though they represent only five to ten percent of the Budapest population. In both Budapest and Szeged, Roma were checked more often without any grounds than non-Roma; and in Szeged, like Budapest, only 18 percent of stops produced a positive result.

Chart 22:

Hungary: Efficiency of stops by ethnicity (September 2007–March 2008)

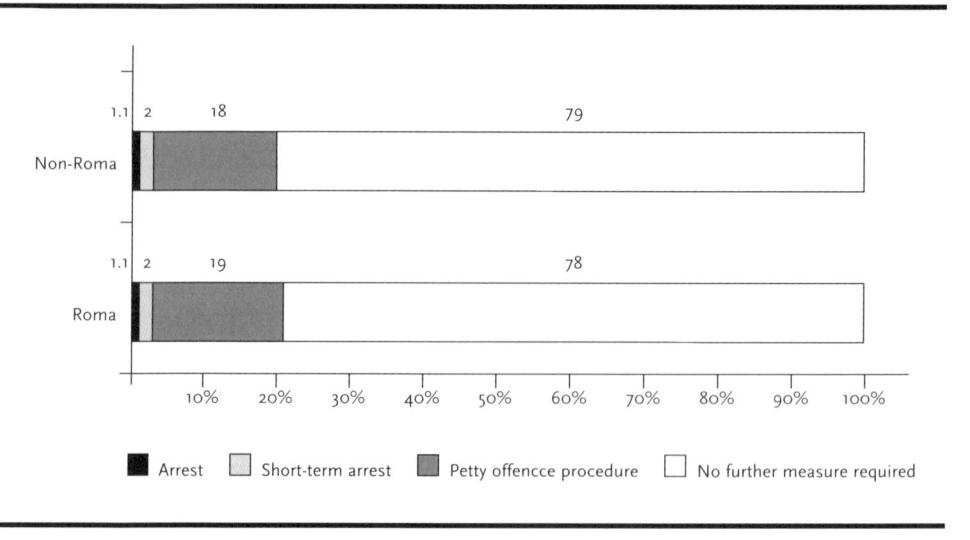

Ethnicity	Arrest	Short-term arrest	Petty offence procedure	No further measure required
Non-Roma	1.1	2	18	79
Roma	1.1	2	19	78

The data from Hungary clearly show that police are engaging in ethnic profiling against Roma, and that this discrimination leads to inefficient policing.

BULGARIAN DATA

While the project design in Bulgaria did not vary from Spain or Hungary, the evaluation of data revealed serious problems. Data review showed that only approximately 30 percent of stops were recorded on the STEPSS stop forms. This number is too low to provide a reliable reflection of stop patterns in the Bulgarian pilot sites. The failure of officers to record their stops, and the fact that this non-compliance went unnoticed until the final evaluation, highlights both problems in project design and implementation, and structural issues within the Bulgarian Police. These problems hold some valuable lessons for Bulgaria and the STEPSS project more broadly.

The evaluation highlighted a number of structural problems in the Directorate of Police. Police managers stated that the Bulgarian police's militarized character would aid project implementation: when instructed, officers would complete the stop forms. In practice, the hierarchy was a hindrance. Senior officers in the Security Police (which oversees patrol officers) supported the project enthusiastically, but while in theory central level decisions are mandatory for subordinates, in practice the patrol officers of the Security Police operate under the command of Area Police Departments (APDs) and their subordinate District Police Directorates (DPDs). Orders have to pass through the chain of command. STEPSS coordinators failed to engage directly with the directors of the APDs and line supervisors, and these officers failed to understand or support the project and resisted its implementation. They could do this with little concern for adverse consequences as there are no serious penalties for non-execution of an order for either district police commanders or patrol officers. Bulgarian policing has no culture of measuring productivity or of holding officers accountable for performance. A project introducing greater oversight was predictably resisted, and the lack of accountability mechanisms meant that there was little that senior officers in the central Security Police could do to rectify the problems.

The project's effort to adapt practices from the U.K. to a Bulgarian context failed to adequately account for the local context and its very different policing culture. For example, the stop form was detailed and complex (though the check-box structure was easier to complete than existing forms) and it had to be completed in addition to existing paperwork. This created significant additional work; in some cases as many as three forms had to be filled out, in addition to entering the data from the STEPSS form into a computer. This could take as much as 30 to 40 minutes for a single stop, an issue that was raised repeatedly during the post-project evaluation. In addition, line supervisors did not check officer compliance. Patrol officers did not hand in their stop forms daily, but kept the entire pad of forms until completed. As radio logs are only kept for a short period, it was impossible to cross-reference forms and radio logs to verify accuracy at the end of the project. There was also no mechanism for reviewing and correcting incomplete forms.

A series of problems with the database software and difficulties connecting the database to pilot stations led to a three month delay and backlog in data entry. Lack of computer skills meant that data entry was slow;[64] the APDs eventually hired external data entry staff, but the delay meant that stop data were not available for analysis and discussion to either local police managers or to community members during the project, nor did officer non-compliance become clear until the project had ended.

V. The STEPSS Process

As previously outlined, STEPSS was designed as a common process for three countries, the elements of which were adapted to local conditions. This chapter reviews key principles and models for the process, with reflections on adaptations and lessons learned. The next sections follow a rough chronological order of the STEPSS project, from the policy and practice assessment and the U.K. study tour, to examining community engagement strategies, developing the stop form and operational protocols, training, supervision, and data analysis.

1. Assessing Police Policy and Practices

STEPSS began with a policy audit,[65] to review existing law, policy, and practice. Existing policies and training practices regarding the use of police powers to stop and search were examined in each setting. The assessment identified policies and practices likely to produce disproportionate impacts on ethnic minority and immigrant communities. It also reviewed previously-collected data on identity checks, stops and searches, and arrests; data recording practices; and how data were used to inform operations.[66] The assessment provided basic information necessary to develop the stop form, operational guidelines, and a training package for the STEPSS pilot program.

It was important to conduct the assessment at each pilot site; even when law and policy is national in scope, local policing units often develop their own policies and practices that will affect the implementation of any initiative. For example, police in Szeged, Hungary, had a well developed system of recording stops and using the data to determine performance. This facilitated STEPSS implementation as shown in the high compliance rate at this pilot site.

2. Learning from Experience: Understanding, Commitment, and "Buy-in"

STEPSS required police to change their practices and rethink how to use stops, and to consider the impacts of stops on different communities. For the process to function effectively, it is important that both the police and the community understand the nature of the problem, and accept that there are alternative approaches which offer important benefits as well as challenges.

Each STEPSS partner country had a different impetus for participating. The Hungarian police were still recoiling from the criticism and public mistrust that resulted from their heavy-handed management of demonstrations during the 2007 political crisis in Budapest. As a result, the national police were open to initiatives that could address the collapse in public confidence. Spanish municipal police were already starting to address ethnic profiling at the local level on their own initiative in response to increasingly diverse immigrant populations, and welcomed technical support. In both the Mossos d'Equadra and the Bulgarian National Police, senior officers recognized the potential for discriminatory policing and viewed data gathering to monitor the impact and effectiveness of stops as part of a broader commitment to modern approaches and community policing.

STEPSS was fortunate in having resources to invite police and community members from pilot sites to visit the U.K. at the start of the initiative, to see how the British police and communities have developed their approach to address disproportionate stop and search practices. An introductory conference in London was followed by visits to the London Metropolitan Police Service and the Leicestershire Constabulary. These visits provided direct exposure to systems to record and supervise the use of stops, and community engagement models. Participants also took part in "ride-alongs" during which they witnessed stops in person. The Metropolitan Police Service also offered a "key encounter" training session, where a diverse group of community members and police officers were led through a structured discussion featuring community members reflecting on the experience of being stopped and their perceptions of the police. The U.K. police also spoke candidly about the challenges of conducting stops and searches.

The study tour was a costly activity that will not always be an option for those interested in addressing ethnic profiling. But it is worth noting that in addition to the "full immersion" learning provided, the week-long experience forged valuable relationships among members of the country teams, many of whom—police officers and minority community representatives—had little prior knowledge of each others' worlds. After they returned home, the police participants proved enthusiastic ambassadors for the project. One officer in Hungary complained, "After the captain got back from the study tour all we heard about for weeks was 'this is how they do it in the U.K.'"

British officers provided additional technical assistance following the study tour through visits to each of the project countries. On these visits, the small group of two or three officers would describe their experiences and discuss them with their local colleagues. These visits were scheduled during the final phases of development of the stop form and operational guidance in order to provide a peer review process for the local team. The British officers visited each pilot site and discussed their experiences with local police and community members.

STEPSS would not have been possible without the firm commitment to the project by the police leadership in each force. But it also became clear that project goals must be understood and accepted by police officers at all levels—most critically, by mid-level local commanders and line supervisors. The problems that arise when such understanding is absent were clearest in Bulgaria. Senior officers from central headquarters took part in the study tour rather than pilot site commanders (as was the case with the Spanish and Hungarian participants) and, despite their commitment, there was inadequate "trickle-down" to the pilot sites. During the evaluation, it became clear that police managers at the Bulgarian pilot sites had only a general familiarity with project goals, and could not articulate them fluently. None of the local police saw STEPSS as a means to improve community–police relations, and few perceived it as a means to strengthen supervision of patrol officers. There was a clear lack of local ownership rather, STEPSS was viewed as an imposition; a factor that directly contributed to non-compliance and lack of results in Bulgaria.

Project buy-in also presented problems for the Mossos d'Equadra in Girona. At the time of implementation, the Mossos d'Esquadra was expanding its role in Catalunya, including opening new police stations and taking over some responsibilities previously held by the Spanish National Police. Many Mossos officers were new and relatively inexperienced; officers were frequently reassigned from one station to another; and command structures were also changing. This meant that a number of senior officers who were supportive of the project and received the initial training were moved during the pilot program and that all officers were overextended. Coincidentally, STEPSS came on the heels of a scandal in which Mossos officers had been taped on closed circuit cameras severely beating an immigrant in custody. Thus, while senior commanders viewed STEPSS as a means to improve relations with immigrant communities, lower-level officers saw the project as a control mechanism that questioned their professionalism and implied that they were all racists. This perception compromised their buy-in, which was reflected in negative postings on the police intranet, and in resistance to using the stop form. Furthermore, officers viewed STEPSS as a temporary pilot process to be tolerated for six months, and then abandoned.

> **Key Lessons**
>
> *Understanding*: Clarity about project principles, objectives, activities, potential challenges and potential benefits is essential for all participants. It is important that officers at all levels understand the project benefits both in improved relations with the local community and in providing greater operational effectiveness and management tools.
>
> *Commitment*: The commitment of senior and mid-level officers is vital as they must both "sell" the project to their subordinates as well as implement it.
>
> *"Buy-in"*: All patrol officers as well as supervisors and managers must at a minimum accept (though preferably support) the project and its legitimacy, as they bear the burden of the increased workload.

3. Increasing Community Participation

The primary goal of STEPSS is to improve police relations with minority communities. In this effort, the police and local residents are equal stakeholders and partners in the implementation process. Community participation and transparency are essential aspects of STEPSS—otherwise the project would simply provide police with a new management tool, without benefiting local minority residents. The STEPSS design included comprehensive outreach to identify local civil society groups that could serve as partners in the project. Project plans called for direct community involvement in the project's design and execution, including developing the stop forms and operational guidance, drafting "know your rights" booklets, advising and delivering training, and, most critically, forming the consultation groups that would meet to review the stop data on a regular basis.

STEPSS faced considerable difficulties in creating and maintaining consultative groups in Bulgaria, a challenge that was compounded by the lack of police commitment and the project's results. In Sofia, area residents were highly transitory and the community contained a number of different Roma subgroups; factors which delayed the selection of commonly-recognized local community leaders. In Haskovo, the initial community representative had to be replaced half-way through the pilot program. The new leader, a woman, managed to attract other community members to the consultative group, despite the fact that contacts with the police are typically considered a "male job." Unfortunately, the participation of a male Roma community member who had good connections and authority in the community proved problematic when project coordinators discovered that he was the local loan shark. In Plovdiv, by contrast, leadership of and participation in the consultation group was consistent, with good relations between the police and residents of the local Sheker and Arman Roma neighborhoods.

Spanish partners developed two distinct models of community participation. In Fuenlabrada, a small group of people drawn from local immigrant groups and human rights organizations was established at the start of the process. They helped in project design and training, and took part in regular monthly meetings at which they reviewed stop data with the police. Through this group, police forged relationships with communities they had not previously contacted, with benefits beyond monitoring the stop data. During early meetings, members of the Chinese community reported a series of break-ins to small businesses; they had not reported these due to lack of contact with police and understanding of the justice system. The police responded with visits to explain crime reporting processes and provide guidance on how to improve security. On another occasion, the police were planning an operation in an area with a large Moroccan population; they first reached out through members of the consultative group to seek support for the operation, explaining the limited scope and intensive nature of the action. Fuenlabrada police leaders are planning to broaden the scope of the consultation group, creating an "inter-cultural forum" to discuss a range of community issues, while continuing the work of the STEPSS committee on a quarterly rather than monthly basis.

In Girona, UNESCO Catalunya led community outreach by bringing a large number of groups from Girona and outlying areas to the community meetings. At the meetings, police managers explained the project and took questions and comments. But the Girona police partners and UNESCO decided against sharing extensive data from the stop forms at these meetings, both because they felt the forum was not conducive to discussing sensitive data and because the participants clearly wanted to discuss broader questions. The meetings did facilitate dialogue between the police and immigrant associations which had had little prior contact.

There are inherent tensions in attempting to produce social change through a short-term project. For STEPSS, the most prominent challenge was introducing new practices from outside or above, because achieving sustainable change requires that the local communities engage with and drive new practices and policies. STEPSS clearly demonstrated that ethnic profiling is taking place and directly affects local minority populations, yet this issue was not articulated by local minority communities in the pilot sites. In the United Kingdom and the United States, the outcry against ethnic profiling has been driven by communities victimized by discriminatory policing; the STEPSS project relied on police forces that were willing—for a variety of reasons—to address the issue proactively.

The lack of "bottom-up" pressure for change should not be understood to mean that profiling is not a concern to these communities. New immigrant communities in Spain, and disenfranchised Roma communities in Bulgaria and Hungary, are keenly aware of police profiling, but they are also fighting for equal access to employment, housing, and education—bread and butter issues that have taken precedence to date. An additional factor that bears on this equation is the culture of policing that prevails in each STEPSS country. To varying degrees, Bulgaria, Hungary, and Spain are characterized by state-centered, command-driven policing traditions, with little history of police-community dialogue. In the case of Spain's immigrant communities, residents also bring expectations of policing derived from sometimes abusive policing practices in their countries of origin.

Key Lessons

Equal partnership: Police and residents were joint stakeholders in the STEPSS effort to increase the effectiveness and accountability of police stops. The community must be equal partners in these processes.

Transparency: Without community participation and transparency in each step of the process, the project potentially provides police with a management tool which does not necessarily benefit minority communities.

Organize from the start: Local immigrant and minority communities must be engaged from the very beginning of the process and included in all key aspects.

Representation: Individual community representatives cannot be expected to speak for whole communities. Efforts should be made to draw participants from as many different backgrounds as possible, including different sexes, ages, ethnic and religious groups, local interest groups, or neighborhood associations.

Dialogue and accountability: Data must be shared with the community groups to maintain interest and participation and ensure genuine accountability

Responsiveness: The police must respond to people's concerns and issues raised during dialogue.

Community engagement takes time and energy. Yet this is an essential aspect of initiatives to address ethnic profiling. Community input can assist police in reading and understanding the meaning of their data, and the trust that is built can provide direct results in terms of cooperation in identifying and resolving local safety issues. A next step in community engagement would be to undertake qualitative monitoring whereby the community consultation group works with the police to review the treatment of people during stops.

CIVILIAN MONITORING IN HUNGARY

Responding to the crisis of public confidence in the Hungarian police, the project opted for a system of civilian monitoring of stops as the appropriate form of community engagement. In each pilot site, a team of representatives from the local Roma community observed two shifts a week, and discussed their observations with police supervisors. Community members attended the U.K. study tour, participated in the same training sessions and briefing sessions as the police, and signed confidentially agreements. Police officers were given additional guidelines on safety when on patrol with civilian monitors. The monitors observed all aspects of daily policing, focusing primarily on stops. They had the right to interact with the person being stopped and record any observations on the STEPSS form. They observed the reason for stops, who was being stopped, the conduct of the stop, and ensured that stops were being recorded.

Prior to STEPSS, many Hungarian officers had little contact with Roma. The civilian monitors have opened a door for a frank discussion with Roma community members about patterns of offending, cultural traditions, and other matters. This led to recognition of the need for more training; and in one pilot site, a civilian monitor led a series of training sessions on these issues. The learning has gone both ways: all of the civilian monitors said they developed a new perspective on policing and the challenges police face. As one monitor said:

> *It was good to see how the police work. The officers often asked our opinions, which I appreciated, and they gave me lots of information about the law. I felt like it was a good exchange. It was very good that we got to know each other and were actually having a relationship. I cannot say anything bad about the practices as all I saw was wholly positive. I had preconceptions about the police at the beginning and they were changed by the project—I enjoyed spending time with them, it was a pleasure to be involved.*

Maybe most remarkably, one civilian monitor has joined the police; he will be the first Roma police officer in that district. He began officer training in

September 2008 and runs specific training courses for his colleagues on Roma history and culture.

Officers have gained greater understanding of the experience of being stopped. In the words of one officer:

> I learned a lot from the Roma observer and they learned a lot about police work and the challenges that we face. I also understand, as [one community representative] said that when he is in the underground he gets stopped, but if there are five officers, he gets stopped five times, once by every officer, just because he is a Roma. Anyone would be unhappy with that.

Senior officers spoke positively about unexpected benefits of external oversight. In one case, criminal charges were brought against a police officer for excessive use of force; the civilian monitor was summoned as a witness, and testified that it was a false complaint.

The process also faced challenges. Initially, many police officers voiced safety concerns about the presence of civilians in their vehicles, and reluctance to have a civilian observer with them. In one pilot site, the monitors were often kept waiting for several hours before officers would take them on patrol, and when they did go on patrol, officers would not conduct stops, so there was nothing to observe. This happened on ten of the first sixteen shifts. The problem was corrected after an official complaint to the area commander. Generally, the quality of stops was improved by the presence of monitors. It is clear that officers adapted their behavior to some extent in the presence of monitors, and found ways to evade scrutiny. We know of at least one occasion when an officer stopped but did not ticket a Roma man, but sought out the same man the following day with no observer present, and gave him a fine.

"KNOW YOUR RIGHTS" BOOKLETS AND COMMUNITY OUTREACH

Citizens must know their rights if officers are to be held accountable for their conduct. This is particularly important when introducing stop forms as the residents need to be aware that a form should be completed and that they will receive a copy. Particularly in communities with language differences and mistrust of police, residents need to understand that the form is not a fine or summons. In communities where low literacy is an issue, local radio and other media should be explored as a complementary means of notifying residents of the initiative and of their rights.

STEPSS community consultation groups supported the design of "Know Your Rights" leaflets for distribution in pilot areas, and to be handed out by police to the people they stop. The leaflet should be kept simple and translated into languages commonly used by local residents.

Bulgaria illustrates some of the issues that can arise with limited information about project actions and objectives. Only 500 leaflets were printed for pilot sites with a total Roma population of over 20,000; few complementary information campaigns came to fruition. Police officers reported that people, and particularly ethnic minorities, responded to the stop forms with confusion or fear, with questions such as *"What should I do with this thing now?"* apparently reflecting the belief that the form was court summons or fine. This problem was exacerbated by patrol officers who were unable to explain the form and its purpose, or refused to write their name or sign the form. The experience was not uniformly negative; some officers also met with positive responses and interest in the officer's explanation of the stop form.

4. Developing the Stop Form and Operational Guidance

The basic tool for gathering data was a stop form for officers to complete every time they stopped someone. Each project teams adopted its own approach to the development of the stop form and accompanying guidance. In Girona, Spain, a working group made up of the project coordinator, police, participants from the police training college, Centro UNESCO, and community members met monthly to discuss developments and assign tasks. In Fuenlabrada, Spain, the police developed the recording mechanisms and then reviewed it with project partners and community members through the consultation group. Similar approaches were taken in Hungary and Bulgaria, where they faced complaints from the community members and NGOs about inadequate engagement in the initial design stage.

The four basic purposes of a stop form are to: (1) detect any disproportionality in stops of minority citizens; (2) chart how stops are being used by officers (reasons for stops, suspicion, location, and outcomes); (3) provide a tool for enhanced police supervision; and (4) provide a tool for monitoring of police stops by the community.

The stop forms were loosely based on the British form, but adapted to local contexts. In general the forms collected the following information:

- Personal data of the person stopped (name, age, social security number, address)

- Ethnicity and/or nationality
- Name of the officer conducting the stop
- Time, date, and place of stop
- Legal grounds for the stop
- Open field to record grounds for suspicion
- Outcome (no action, fine, arrest, warning, etc.)
- Additional space to describe more specific situations (e.g., stops of several persons or an incident, descriptions of clothing, other information that might be useful for intelligence purposes).

The stop forms differed considerably in design and complexity. Hungary had the simplest form and Bulgaria the longest. The Bulgarian stop form proved excessively complex, and much of the additional information collected was redundant.[67] Both the Bulgarian and Hungarian police were also still legally required to complete existing forms as well as the STEPSS form during the pilot program. In response, the Hungarian project teams devised a very simple form to minimize the additional paperwork; data collection was also limited to comply with Hungary's very strict personal data protection laws.

In every case, project teams consulted with national data protection offices to be sure that the stop forms did not violate national and European standards.

In Bulgaria and Spain, once officers completed the stop form they were required to give a copy to the person stopped. Research shows that the two biggest sources of dissatisfaction among those stopped are not being given a reason for the stop, and the conduct of officers during the stop.[68] Requiring officers to give a copy of the form to each person they stop means the officer must articulate the reason for the stop. Because the copy of the stop form includes information on citizens' rights and how to complain if they are dissatisfied with the treatment, this also leads the officers to focus on their treatment of the person during the stop.[69]

The clear definition of terms is essential to creating an effective stop form. Data on ethnicity are at the heart of the stop form, and must be recorded in order to capture any disproportionality. Given past abuses of ethnic data and ongoing sensitivities, the question of how to define and record ethnicity must be addressed with sensitivity. The U.K. stop form features 16 "ethnic" categories, as well as "other," and the person stopped is asked to self-identify according to these categories. The officer can also provide his/her perception of the person's ethnicity if they disagree with the self identification.

Bulgaria used the U.K. dual system; while officers' reported some discomfort with asking people to identify their ethnicity, the lack of reliable data in Bulgaria precludes further assessment of what issues arose with this approach. The Hungarian team used officer perception only and established very simple ethnic categories to avoid confusion and enhance data accuracy. In practice, this worked well.

Spain provides useful insights into the challenges of ethnic identification on stop forms. The Fuenlabrada team decided to use nationality as a proxy for ethnicity because—with the exception of the relatively few immigrants who have acquired Spanish citizenship—ethnic minorities are non-nationals. The only group not captured in this categorization is *Gitanos* (Spanish Roma). The Girona team opted to use both nationality and officer perception of ethnic appearance. Their decision reflected a desire to capture the officers' perception, on the grounds that this is more revealing about potential prejudices that may be driving stops. The categories were developed by the working group and reflected local understanding of ethnic groups. Initial data analysis revealed a very close association between nationality and perceived ethnicity, so the final analysis used nationality for purposes of comparison with Fuenlabrada.

While the use of nationality functions at this time in Spain, and will do so in other European countries where immigration is a recent phenomenon and/or where few migrants or their children have nationalized, this approach will become less effective over time. Future efforts to combat profiling will require ethnic rather than nationality-based categorizations. Each community must determine the appropriate ethnic categories in context; but it is worth noting that ethnic categories are fluid and not always self-evident, and it is important to allow that they may evolve over time.[70]

In addition to ethnic categorization, further data collection issues arose around recording the reason for stops—specifically, whether to record the law under which the person was stopped, or the type of police operation that led to the stop. Comparing the experience in Fuenlabrada (which recorded the police operation) and Girona (which recoded the law in question, as did Bulgaria), it appears that information on the type of police operation provides a far more useful analytical tool for police management purposes, because the police can change operational practices, but not the law.

Key Lessons

Keep it simple: Because the introduction of stop forms will increase officers' workload, it is important to find a way to minimize the burden.

Provide clear operational guidelines: Assist officers in understanding and articulating grounds for stops, without providing ready-made answers for open fields on reasons for suspicion.

Be clear about what variables you want to collect on a form and why.

Use the form to give a message to those stopped: Requiring officers to give a person a copy of the form encourages the development of grounds for suspicion and enhances accountability, especially when the form includes information on rights and responsibilities and complaints procedures.

Think ahead about data entry: Plan procedures and assign responsibilities for data entry, and test any new data systems in advance.

Comply with data protection standards

Establishing a clear definition of the "hit rate" is also critical. The United Kingdom defines hits as arrests. Fuenlabrada included administrative outcomes as well as arrests, but only included outcomes of stops initiated by officers as hits. In Girona, forms included officers' stops of people they witnessed committing a criminal or administrative offense; similar categories were used in Hungary, but a broad definition of offenses are captured in the "*in flagrante*" category under their petty offenses law. These differences mean that hit rates are not easily comparable across different policing districts or countries. The hit rate is, nonetheless, an essential measure of efficiency and must be collected.

The inclusion of an additional open field for recording specific grounds for suspicion is a valuable tool for supervision. Officers often had difficulty articulating grounds for suspicion. Training made available through the STEPSS project helped officers address this question (training is discussed further in Section 5, below).

5. Training[71]

STEPSS required police officers to adopt new practices representing a new philosophy in local policing. Training was essential to build understanding of project objectives and benefits, as well as to teach officers how to complete the forms and enter the data.

Project design called for joint training of police with community members, to support community representatives' understanding of the project and ability to understand the data, as well as their ability to address the conduct of stops.

The policy and practice assessments at the start of the project found that all of the forces had some form of diversity training. The impact of diversity training is contested by experts, based on arguments that it can stigmatize particular ethnic groups or simply revisit rather than correct ethnic stereotypes.[72] Two principles guided the STEPSS approach to training: first, that the community should be directly involved in the design and delivery of training and tailor information to specific local groups and issues; and second, that police training works best when it is directly related to legal standards and practical aspects of policing. STEPSS project guidance recommended the following elements:

- Introduction to the project's origins and objectives, the concept of ethnic profiling, and practices that generate disproportionality in stops (noting that profiling may be either individual and/or structural/institutional).
- Practical guidance on the law and how to complete a stop form.
- Guidance on the conduct of a stop and interactive training with community members on the experience of being stopped.
- Provision by community members of basic information about local issues.
- Practical guidance on grounds of suspicion that do not rely on ethnicity, and how to make more effective stops.

The Hungarian training closely followed this pattern. The guidance on suspicion was developed and delivered by a "cop's cop," an experienced and well-respected officer who was able to drive the issue home without alienating patrol officers. This enhanced officer buy-in. The Hungarian Helsinki Committee project coordinator also attended many of the patrol officers' daily briefing sessions at police stations in pilot areas. In project evaluation interviews, all officers demonstrated a clear understanding of the project's logic and objectives.

The training in Bulgaria consisted of two modules only: (1) a one-day training on the stop forms and data software system for two senior officers from each department; and (2) a two-hour lecture on project objectives, stop forms, and operational guidance attended by a third of the patrol officers in each pilot site. Community representatives attended the lectures, but not the training on the database software system, nor were they included in the design or delivery of training. Training did not address the conduct of stops, nor did daily briefings for patrol officers provide any refresher training. In Sofia, where there was a high turnover of officers, newly recruited staff were not informed about STEPSS nor taught how to use the forms. These limitations contributed to failure to gather adequate data, and other problems discussed elsewhere in this report. Most regrettable was the lost opportunity to work with the community to develop a greater understanding of the impact of ID checks on those stopped and learn more about the culture, experiences, and needs of their local communities.

The two Spanish pilot sites had contrasting models of training. In both areas, all project partners cooperated closely in developing and delivering the training, which was fairly similar in content. However, police officers' reactions were quite different. In Fuenlabrada, the entire corps attended and were generally receptive to and positive about the training, which provided: (1) an introduction to the project and the British experience; (2) a definition of stops and searches and a review of relevant law; (3) a participatory exercise to sensitize officers to discrimination; (4) a lecture from Amnesty International and SOS Racismo; and (5) a review of the STEPSS protocols and forms.

The positive reaction of officers in Fuenlabrada is likely due to factors including the relative youth of the Fuenlabrada municipal police, their pride in being innovators, and their confidence in their managers. It is also noteworthy that the training presented STEPSS as an initiative to improve policing services and efficiency. The police leadership also made it clear that they had made a commitment beyond the project itself and planned to implement STEPSS as a permanent policy.

In Girona, both police managers and patrol officers attended the training. The course covered: (1) introduction to STEPSS; (2) community relations; (3) improving the quality of police-citizen encounters; and (4) the law on stop powers and the stop form. Despite the strong commitment at the leadership level, there was considerable resistance to the training and STEPSS project in the municipal police and, most markedly, in the Mossos d'Esquadra. While much of the resistance reflected external factors (as discussed above in Section 2), trainers also offered some specific reflections and suggestions for improving training. The training session opened with discussions of discrimination and disproportionality, which put officers on the defensive—in contrast to the reaction when presented with stop forms as a tool for improving police services. One trainer remarked that, in retrospect, it would be good to do the pilot program first and then, on the basis of the data demonstrating disproportionality and benefits to police productivity, only afterwards relate the practice to discrimination and a discussion of the influence of stereotypes. Another trainer felt that it would be better not to have the discrimination training conducted by persons of ethnic minority origin as it enabled officers to view their contributions as personal testimonial and not see the minority trainers as serious professionals.[73] Trainers agreed that officers accepted the general discussion of discrimination and the challenges of immigrant integration, but that resistance appeared when these were related to specific policing practices. Some suggested separating the two aspects, having policing practices and practical guidance on the stop form presented on one day and discrimination on another.

Key lessons

Joint teaching and learning: Both police and community members need training, and both have important perspectives to impart. At least some joint training should be conducted to establish a clear message about values, objectives, and procedures.

Training content: Trainings must cover (1) using stop powers: operational guidance on developing suspicion for stops based on intelligence rather than ethnic stereotyping, improving the quality of encounters, and completing the stop form, and (2) basic information about the different ethnic and religious communities within a local area, their needs and priorities, and the experience of being stopped.

Delivery: Specific aspects of training are best delivered by those with the most credibility for their audience, such as a well-respected police officer.

Interactive training techniques: Training packages should be practical, interactive, and include all participants in discussions, scenarios, and role playing.

Training must be on-going – and repeated for those that miss it or in briefing sessions.

6. Supervision

The oversight and direction that patrol officers receive from their line supervisors and managers are critical to the quality of their work, both in terms of accountability and effectiveness. The STEPSS project provided a memorandum on different approaches to obtaining officer compliance with the requirement that they complete stop forms,[74] and country partners adopted different elements in each setting.

Fuenlabrada achieved excellent officer compliance with STEPSS protocols, and went further, using the data as a management tool more broadly (see following box). Sequentially numbered forms allowed every stop to be traced to an individual officer; supervisors could easily observe when forms were not submitted or submitted out of sequence. Police managers also checked the numbers of stop forms against radio logs (officers are required to call in during stops). Forms with missing or problematic information were returned to the officer to complete in full, and only when the supervisor signed off on the form was it entered into the database.

Supervisors from both the municipal police and the Mossos d'Esquadra also checked the forms from each shift and required officers to complete information as required; they too cross checked numbers against radio logs. Delays in data analysis, discussed in the next section, precluded further use of the stop data for management purposes in Girona.

In Bulgaria, lack of commitment and understanding were seen in the failure to develop any local guidance on compliance. Supervisors failed to notice that their officers were not filling out the stop forms until the end of the project. Here also the problem was exacerbated by delays in development of the database and data entry. Supervisors never saw the data as a relevant or beneficial tool of either supervision or management.

STOP DATA AS A MANAGEMENT TOOL IN FUENLABRADA

In Fuenlabrada, the stop data were used to strengthen police supervision and management. Officers initially had problems completing the open field for suspicion, and guidelines were produced that included a list of reasons for stops and examples of what grounds would be acceptable within each category. This provided guidance, while still requiring the officer to articulate a reason for his/her suspicions in each case.

Most importantly, the sergeant in charge of STEPSS analyzed the data monthly, and the data on the type of stop and "motivation" allowed senior officers to supervise individual officers' use of stops more closely. For example, they were concerned with stops in the categories of "other" or "attitude or suspicious behavior" as these are areas in which officers have most discretion to act on stereotypes or negative generalizations. Supervisors first ensured that officers understood the different categories and the type of stops that fell into each; this resulted in a reduction of officers recording "other" on the forms. The free field for recording "motivation" then allowed senior officers to monitor the reasons given for stops under "attitude and suspicious behavior" category to ensure they were satisfied that the threshold of "motivation" had been met.

More broadly, senior officers could assess the use of stops across the force and use data from the forms to guide personnel deployment. Although most crimes and anti-social behavior take place on the weekend, the forms showed that most stops were being made on Wednesdays. Officers (like everyone else) like to have the weekends off and had managed their schedules to work more on weekdays.

Similarly, when managers plotted stops by time of day for October, they found peaks and troughs in the numbers of stops through each day, including points in the day when few or no stops were conducted at all—showing that officers were all taking their breaks at the same times. Managers restructured break times to make sure that officers were available at all times. Data from subsequent months showed more even stop patterns.

In Hungary, all the supervisors checked stop forms at the end of each shift. Supervisors also reported that they conducted periodic spot checks, visiting officers on patrol or accompanying patrols not only to see that forms were filled out, but also to assess the conduct of stops. At the close of the data gathering, it became clear that only 68 percent of stops had been recorded. This speaks to the ingenuity of officers and their ability to evade scrutiny. It also indicates the need to examine supervisory approaches and develop more effective techniques. None of the officers interviewed for the evaluation reported being "spot checked" so we do not know how well this worked. Despite these weaknesses, Hungarian police supervisors found the exercise to be useful. In the words of a police Captain from Kaposvár:

> "We might continue this, because before we didn't know how to supervise the conduct of stops. It has highlighted all sorts of information that we didn't know before. Supervision definitely needs to be emphasized more within the Hungarian police force as traditionally stops have been used by officers to show that they were doing something during their shifts. The idea was that the more you do, the harder you are working. We need to change this mindset."

Key Lessons

Supervision is crucial to achieving compliance with recording stops, improving officers targeting of stops and effectiveness, and enhancing the quality of stops. Police supervisors should routinely review the reasons officers give for carrying out stops, identity checks and searches. Strategies for supervision include of review of individual stops and analysis of aggregate patterns of officers' stops.

Provide specific training to all police managers and supervising officers on the use of stop forms for supervision and management.

Use a variety of supervision techniques such as a mandatory review of stop forms at the end of every shift, comparing numbers of forms submitted with radio calls logging stops, and direct observation of patrol officers and their conduct

Data supports supervision when it is available on a regular basis and can be compared to operational dynamics and personnel assignments for the period.

7. Data Analysis

Data analysis proved a project weak point. STEPSS contracted criminologists and statisticians in each country to analyze the data. However, for a number of reasons, including slow data entry and other logistical factors, the analysts only fully processed the data at the end of the project period. Furthermore, once analyzed, the data had to be extensively revised, corrected and concepts such as odds ratios introduced. This revealed both the challenge of analyzing stop data, and the failure of the approach taken by STEPSS project management in guiding partners on key elements of stop data analysis.[75] The chart below on the facing page sets out the basic indicators that should be measured and analyzed through data collection. It highlights the information that each variable will provide—both in terms of proportionality and fairness, and as a police management tool for increasing overall effectiveness.

In Fuenlabrada, the sargeant in charge of STEPSS was adept with accounting software and undertook his own independent data analysis. The Fuenlabrada Municipal Police had monthly data in easy to understand formats that they shared with the community, and used in supervision and management. As prior discussions have made clear, regular data analysis is key to reaping the benefits of gathering stop data. Proper data analysis helps identify causes of disproportionality and reduce it, and also improves police supervision and management.

Key Lessons

Stop data should be analyzed on a frequent and regular basis in order to match trends in stops with specific security issues and operational directives. Additional training may be required for police managers and community representatives on how to read the stop data produced, what questions to ask and how to respond to operational issues that arise.

Stop data analysis is not easy, particularly when concepts of profiling and disproportionality are first introduced. Once a conceptual grasp is established, data analysis can be done in-house by police staff.

Timely data input and monthly analysis are essential to extract maximum benefit from the data as a supervisory and management tool.

Table 7:

Key indicators for stop data analysis

Indicator/data to be measured	Objective	Commentary: Fairness and proportionality	Commentary: Data as police management tool
Number of stops by nationality, ethnic group, age, and gender compared to their proportion in the resident population.	Identify disproportionate stops of immigrants/ ethnic minorities, both force-wide and by individual officers, specialized units, or shifts.	Analyze overall numbers of stops and the percentage of stops of immigrants/ ethnic minorities, and whether this is disproportionate compared to their proportion of the local population.	Provides basic information on the work of individual officers, units, shifts, or zones, and patterns for the entire police force. Gives the number of stops each officer is making, and allows supervisors to determine if individual officers or units are disproportionately targeting certain ethnic or religious groups.
Number of stops leading to searches by nationality, ethnic group, age, and gender compared to the proportion in the resident population.	Identify any disproportionality in searches of immigrants/ ethnic minorities.	Data analysis will look at the overall numbers of stops that lead to searches and determine whether this is disproportionate when compared to the percentage of immigrants or minorities in the local population and apparent involvement in arrestable activity.	Provides basic information about total numbers of searches for each officer or unit; allows supervisors to determine if officers or units are disproportionately targeting certain ethnic or religious groups for searches after stops.
Trend analysis of number of stops and searches over time by nationality, ethnic group, age, and gender.	Identify reasons for any disproportionality in stops and searches.	Determine whether there is a valid operational reason for targeting certain groups at certain times in relation to reported crime trends.	When compared to reported crime rates and other factors, data can show factors driving the use of stops. This data can be cross-referenced with the rates of effectiveness to give an insight into strategic decision-making around special operations.

Indicator/data to be measured	Objective	Commentary: Fairness and proportionality	Commentary: Data as police management tool
Reason for the stop by nationality, ethnic group, age, and gender.	Identify reasons that may indicate stereotypes, improve judgments of suspicion, and targeting of stops on behavior and intelligence. Monitor decision-making processes to determine if they meet legal standards.	Data analysis will show if specific ethnic groups are being targeted for specific crimes. Cross-reference reasons for stops with the positive results and see whether officers are basing their stops on accurate assessments of suspicion.	Provides information about how officers are targeting stops, how many stops are as part of an operation, and how many are based on the individual officer's discretion. Allows managers to check that officers are conducting stops in line with legal standards. Can also check if stops are being targeted at crimes/problems that are of highest priority to the local community.
Number of stops leading to positive results.	Increase the number of stops that produce positive results.	Provides a trend analysis of changes in efficiency and supports effective use of stop powers.	Provides analysis of the effectiveness of stops overall and of specific operations. Allows a comparison of effectiveness of different officers and units within police departments and even between similar police departments. May be used to support training and improvements in intelligence use, to increase effectiveness. The number of arrests in certain areas can also act as an early warning of potential officer bias.

Indicator/data to be measured	Objective	Commentary: Fairness and proportionality	Commentary: Data as police management tool
Number of positive stop results analyzed by nationality or ethnic group.	Reduce disproportionality between unsuccessful stops of immigrants/ ethnic minorities versus unsuccessful stops of nationals/ ethnic majority residents.	Identify where disproportionality reflects offending rates and where lower rates of positive results indicate that stereotypes are influencing stops.	Monitoring disproportionality in the number of unsuccessful stops shows how much time is being wasted targeting ethnic minority groups over other groups.
Relation of different zones within the police district, types of stops and variations in stops of ethnic groups by zone.	Identify any differences in patterns of policing by zones and the impact they have on national/ethnic groups and their overall effectiveness.	Examining the use of stops and disproportionality by zone can identify whether specific operations have a disproportionate impact on certain groups, and whether that is justified by their effectiveness and local crime patterns.	Provides information about levels and focus of police deployments and whether they reflect crime patterns and local priorities.

VI. Conclusions

The U.K. and the United States have grappled with disproportionality in stops and searches over decades and continue to do so. As a fundamental first step, it is necessary to recognize that police use of stops and searches may have a discriminatory impact on ethnic minorities. Beyond this, the process of understanding and changing the factors that drive ethnic profiling is complex and involves culture and practice, institutions, and communities.

STEPSS project partners had the foresight to recognize that they might have a problem with ethnic profiling and were willing to tackle the issue directly and share their experiences. These organizations and individuals undertook an ambitious series of activities over a short project timespan; they have helped to deepen our understanding of the dynamics of ethnic profiling and the ways in which it may be addressed. These achievements, and the challenges faced along the way, have produced valuable lessons both for the pilot sites continuing this work and for others adopting and adapting the STEPSS approach.

STEPSS results confirmed that ethnic profiling is not an exception to the rule, but is in fact the general rule. Results also show that this disproportionality is not justified by different offending rates, confirming similar findings in both the U.K. and United States. Profiling is not effective. It inconveniences large numbers of people and alienates entire groups within the community,[76] to no demonstrable law enforcement purpose. Importantly, STEPSS also shows that it is possible to do something about ethnic profiling, and that monitoring stops and gathering ethnic data are important tools that not only address ethnic profiling, but can also be used to enhance the effectiveness of police use of stops, and contribute to smarter management of police operations and resources. Finally, STEPSS demonstrated that ethnic data gathering can be conducted in full compliance with personal data protection standards.

These results make a powerful argument for the development and use of stop data monitoring in any setting where there is reason to believe that ethnic profiling is prevalent. Where national or local police and/or elected authorities resolve to use these techniques, it is vital that they work in partnership with all stakeholders—that is, with the local community and ethnic minority groups as well as with the police. Community input assists police in reading and understanding the meaning of their data, and builds trust that is shown to directly benefit policing through increasing cooperation in identifying and resolving local safety issues.[77] Without community participation and transparency in each step of the process, the project potentially provides police with a management tool which does not address discrimination or benefit minority communities. Stop data are an accountability tool that should be gathered and shared with local communities to reduce ethnic profiling and enhance community safety.

Annex A

Police Powers to Conduct Stops in STEPSS Partner Countries

STEPSS is focused on police powers to conduct stops and searches. In many cases, this can lead to a request or demand to search the person or the person's vehicle. There are considerable differences among European countries in the legal powers of the police to conduct stops, identity checks and searches, as can be seen in the STEPSS project countries.

Under Bulgarian law,[78] all police officers have the right to carry out stops for a wide range of reasons including suspicion that a person has committed an illegal act, for the investigation of a crime, for the examination of ID documents or residence permits, as part of standard procedure at a police check point, and if requested by another state institution. Searches are permitted whenever a person has been arrested, where there is information that a person carries illegal or dangerous substances, or at a crime scene if there is information that a person has been involved in a crime. Searches of belongings can occur under similar circumstances or when it has not been possible to establish a person's identification or the individual is illegally in the country. Police officers can stop a vehicle to check identification and driving licenses, if there is information that a crime has been committed, or to enforce the Law on Road Traffic.

Bulgarian legislation provides little guidance on what constitutes suspicion to justify the different types of stops. The only provision prohibiting discrimination in police work is found in the Law on the Ministry of the Interior, Instruction I-23 (secondary legislation adopted at the ministerial level), which requires officers to "respect the dignity and rights of all citizens, without discriminating according to age, gender, sexual orientation, race, ethnicity, political views and nationality."[79] The instruction goes on to provide guidelines for the conduct of stops, stating that the officer "must introduce her/himself with rank, family name and name of the structural unit within the police force and that (s)he must show her/his police card and badge upon request."[80] The police currently record their stops on forms that are collated and stored locally. The data are not released nationally. Officers call in stops on their radios if they need to check whether someone is wanted for an offense, but the information is only kept for a short period of time and is not used for statistical analysis.

Hungarian law gives the police wide discretion to stop and search. Article 29 of the 1994 Police Act[81] gives officers full authority to stop and ask for identification of "anyone whose identity needs to be established." The failure of a person to identify himself or cooperate can lead to search and short-term arrest up to 12 hours until the person is identified.[82] The Police shall be entitled to hold arrested persons in public security detention for up to 24 hours if the arrest was necessary for identification.[83] The act declares that identification may need to be established for purposes of public order or safety, crime prevention, crime detection, establishing the legality of residence, traffic control, or if the identity is to be established in the interest of a third party.[84] A search may be conducted if an arrest is taking place or if it is "deemed necessary" for the establishment of a person's identity, if there is suspicion that a person has committed a criminal or petty offense, if it is necessary to prevent "danger," or during raids. Further, Article 44 of the Police Act allows the police to stop vehicles at any time to check the legality of vehicle possession or operation.[85]

The law does not determine a minimum level of suspicion, although Hungarian law includes the concept of "simple suspicion," a concept that remains undefined, in effect allowing officers to search practically anyone at any time. The 2008 amendment to the Police Act requires officers to provide an explanation to the person stopped of the basis for the stop.[86] The Police Act does not refer to discrimination but the Hungarian Constitution has a general antidiscrimination clause that refers to fundamental human and civil rights.[87] A decision of the Constitutional Court has extended the principle of non-discrimination to the whole of the criminal justice system.[88] Furthermore the Police Act contains the requirement of taking measures without any bias[89] and that police shall respect and protect human dignity and safeguard human rights[90]. Officers currently record identity checks on forms submitted to supervisors. Officers are also required to call headquarters in Budapest when they stop someone to check whether the person is wanted. The calls are logged and can provide statistics on numbers of stops.

Spanish law requires police officers to have a "motive" to conduct a stop or search. Exactly what constitutes "motive" remains undefined. The Constitutional Court has ruled that the police have the right to search a person, "within the framework of prevention and investigation of criminal activity," even if there is no indication that the person has committed a crime.[91] The Supreme Court has ruled that stops must be carried out with reasonable care and within the spirit of an investigation; the police can act on simple suspicion but that suspicion cannot be "illogical, irrational or arbitrary."[92] The Law on the Security Forces and Corps states that all police officers must act in all situations with "absolute political neutrality and impartiality, and ... without discrimination based on race, religion or opinion."[93] This requirement is significantly weakened by the 2001 Constitutional Court ruling allowing ethnic profiling in the policing of immigration law.[94]

In the United Kingdom, the 1984 Police and Criminal Evidence Act (PACE) gives police officers the powers to stop and search any person in public when they have reasonable suspicion that the person possesses stolen goods or prohibited articles. Stop and search powers are embodied in a range of legislation that is collectively regulated by the PACE Code of Practice A. The code makes clear that reasonable suspicion cannot be based on personal factors alone and must have an objective basis determined by the circumstances of the individual case. It states:

> Reasonable suspicion can never be supported on the basis of personal factors alone without the supporting intelligence or information. For example, a person's colour, age, hairstyle or manner of dress, or the fact that he is known to have a previous conviction for possession of an unlawful article, cannot be used alone or in combination with each other as the sole basis on which to search that person. Reasonable suspicion cannot be based on generalisations or stereotypical images of certain groups or categories of people as more likely to be involved in criminal activity. A person's religion cannot be considered as reasonable grounds for suspicion and should never be considered as a reason to stop or stop and search an individual.[95]

In addition to clarifying the meaning of reasonable suspicion, the code makes provision for the recording of all stops and searches. Officers are required wherever practicable to provide the person who has been stopped with a record of the encounter, which includes the grounds for the search, the object/s that officers are looking for, the outcome and the name and station of the officer/s conducting the search. The record also contains personal details of the person searched such as name, address, ethnic origin, and a description, all of which the person can refuse to give. Since 1992, the Ministry of Justice has published annual figures on stops and searches conducted in all 43 police forces broken down by, reason for stop, ethnicity, gender and outcome.[96]

Annex B

Hungarian Sampling Design and Methodological Issues

1. Sampling Design

The very high rate of stops in Hungary resulted in a total of 22,375 stop forms being submitted in the three pilot sites. This created prohibitive data entry problems, and the project team agreed to use a proportionate, layered sample of the forms for data analysis purposes. But the sampling process had to overcome several problems.

First, data from the different pilot sites were not fully consistent. In Szeged, data collection was stopped as of March 1, 2008, instead of March 17, 2008. In Kaposvár there was a two-month period in the middle of data gathering during which the officer collecting the forms at the end of each shift discarded forms that were not properly filled out. This situation was corrected after two months. A further difficulty arose because the envelopes in which local police sent in the forms they had gathered were not always accurately dated, and it was not possible in all cases to establish the exact time period or chronology of some stop forms.

To address these issues, and permit trend analysis, project analysts separated the forms with dates from those without dates. They created a sample from the dated group by dividing it into three subgroups with the stop forms in a chronological sequence. Stop forms were selected at random and then every fifth form of this initial sample was selected to constitute the final sample for analysis. Despite the problem with the

Kaposvár data, the high rate of stops meant that the selected sample was still far larger (2,551) than the number required for statistical significance (300 items).

The undated forms were also divided into three sub-groups and then every fifth form was selected at random. Then, the dated and undated samples were combined. The trend analysis used only the dated sample, whereas the aggregate analyses were run on the combined sample.

Table 8:

Hungary: Number of STEPSS forms and forms in the sample

Premises	Budapest	Kaposvár	Szeged	Total
Number of forms	2,015	11,255	9,105	22,375
Number of forms in sample	403	2,251	1,821	4,475

2. Adjustments to data on rate of stops

The rate of stops in Hungary also had to be adjusted to reflect stops in which the STEPSS form was not filled out. The police in the pilot sites provided the total number of stops performed over a seven-month period (September 1, 2007–March 31, 2008) that included the six months of data collection (September 17, 2007–March 17, 2008). The total for the three areas was 43,094 stops.[97]

Table 9:

Hungary: Number of stops during STEPSS period

Premises	Budapest	Kaposvár	Szeged	Total
Number of checks recorded over seven months	3,538	25,770	13,786	43,094

The analysts adjusted the data to estimate a total for six months by calculating the monthly average and multiplying that number by six.

Table 10:

Hungary: Number of stops during six months of STEPSS period

Premises	Budapest	Kaposvár	Szeged	Total
Number of checks	3,033	22,089	11,817	36,939

This number is much higher than the number of STEPSS forms received from the police.

Table 11:
Overall number of ID checks and completed forms within the project period

Area	Number of stops	Percentage of total	Number of forms completed	Percentage of total	Percentage of forms compared to total number of checks
Budapest	3,033*	8	2,015	8	66
Kaposvár	22,089*	60	13,506**	53	61
Szeged	11,817*	32	9,934**	39	84
Total	**36,939***	100	**25,455***	100	69

* Adjusted figure
** Hypothetical figure

In order to establish the compliance rate, the analysts had to calculate the number of STEPSS forms that would have been received had data collection in Kaposvár and Szeged matched project protocols. For Kaposvár, analysts made an assumption that half of the forms were discarded by the supervisor creating a deficit on one month's worth of forms. The 11,255 forms received from Kaposvár were assumed to constitute five months worth of forms, and the corresponding figure for the full six months was assumed to be 13,506 forms. For Szeged, analysts calculated the monthly average number of forms filled out, and added half of one month to the total to make up a full six-month's worth of data. With these adjustments, the totals for actual stops and for the number of STEPSS stop forms completed are as follows.

Annex C

STEPSS Resource Packet

The following materials are available on request from the Open Society Justice Initiative. Please contact: info@justiceinitiative.org.

General
- Guidelines for conducting an assessment of existing law, policy, and operational guidelines
- U.K. study tour agenda
- Stops monitoring tool providing guidance on basic components of gathering and analyzing stop data
- Compliance mechanism memo

Bulgaria
- Stop form (English and Bulgarian)
- Know Your Rights leaflet (English and Bulgarian)
- Operational guidance
- Stops database/data entry user manual (English and Bulgarian)
- National STEPSS report

Hungary
- Stop form (English or Hungarian)
- Know Your Rights booklet
- Operational guidance (English or Hungarian)
- Training syllabus
- National STEPSS report

Spain
- Stop forms from Fuenlabrada and Girona (English or Spanish)
- Know Your Rights booklets (English or Spanish)
- Operational guidance (English or Spanish)
- Training syllabus (English or Spanish)
- Short video about the STEPSS project and ethnic profiling in Fuenlabrada.

Annex D

Ethnic Profiling in Europe: An Overview of the Justice Initiative Project

In 2005, the Open Society Justice Initiative, which works around the globe to foster rights-based law reform, launched an effort to address ethnic profiling by police in Europe. The Justice Initiative was concerned on the one hand by long-standing allegations of police discrimination against Roma and other visible minorities in the course of ordinary crime prevention activities, and on the other by new reports about law enforcement targeting Muslims in the fight against terrorism. Working closely with local partners in various European countries, the Justice Initiative aims to address the current gaps in understanding, documenting, and addressing this problem by pursuing the following goals:

1. Increasing awareness of the issue, in part through research and documentation, among law enforcement officers, human rights advocates, policymakers, and the public;
2. Advocating for the adoption of a clear European norm and national legislation that explicitly ban ethnic profiling in all contexts, including counter-terrorism; and
3. Developing the capacity of civil society and police to work together in creating and applying good practices to monitor and remedy discriminatory patterns.

The following publications are available from the Justice Initiative at www.Justice initiative.org or by emailing a request to info@justiceinitiative.org:

- *Justice Initiatives: Ethnic Profiling in Europe*, June 2005, 99 pages.
- *Ethnic Profiling in the Moscow Metro*, June 2006, 67 pages.
- *"I Can Stop and Search Whoever I Want": Police Stops of Ethnic Minorities in Bulgaria, Hungary and Spain*, April 2006, 106 pages.
- *Ethnic Profiling in the European Union* (working title; publication scheduled for 2009).
- *Ethnic Profiling on the Paris Metro* (working title; publication scheduled for 2009).

Adoption of a clear European norm and national legislation

The Justice Initiative has fostered collaborative relationships with regional networks and NGOs, to raise awareness in European and international institutions of the issue of ethnic profiling and the problems associated with this practice. The issue is beginning to gain recognition, the first step towards establishing a clear European norm. Indicators of progress include:

- The final opinion of the EU network of independent experts on human rights addresses ethnic profiling in detail, concluding that "differential treatment on [grounds of ethnicity] should in principle be considered unlawful under any circumstances."
- In May 2007, Council of Europe Human Rights Commissioner Thomas Hammarberg issued a viewpoint on ethnic profiling which cited the Justice Initiative's work and criticized the use of profiling in counter-terrorism.
- The European Commission against Racism and Intolerance (ECRI, the Council of Europe's anti-racism watchdog) issued General Policy Recommendation No. 11 on police discrimination, which defines and addresses ethnic profiling.
- The European Parliament's Civil Liberties (LIBE) committee is preparing a self-initiated parliamentary report on ethnic profiling in counter-terrorism, law enforcement, immigration, customs, and border control.

The development of civil society and police capacity to address profiling

The STEPSS project has been the most important undertaking to date in our efforts to identify and implement strategies to address ethnic profiling and improve police-minority relations. In addition, the Justice Initiative is currently partnering with the University of Warwick, United Kingdom, to research and draft "Combating Ethnic Profiling; A Handbook of Good Practice" for the European Union Fundamental Rights Agency (FRA). The handbook will be published by the FRA in 2009. It contains examples of good practice from many EU member states, and elaborates a conceptual model of good practice areas.

Notes

1. See, for example, the reports of the European Commission against Racism and Intolerance on Austria (2000); France (1999); Germany (2003); Greece (1999); Hungary (1999 and 2004); Italy (2002); Romania (2001); Spain (2002); Switzerland (2003); and the United Kingdom (2000); among others.

2. *Rosalind Williams*, Spanish Constitutional Court Decision No. 13/2001, January 29, 2001 (STC 13/2001).

3. "[T]he Roma originated from the regions situated between north west India and the Iranian plateau. The first written traces of their arrival in Europe date back to the fourteenth century. Today there are between eight and ten million Roma living in Europe. They are to be found in almost all Council of Europe member States and indeed, in some Central and East European countries, they represent over 5% of the population. The majority of them speak Romani, an Indo-European language that is understood by a very large number of Roma in Europe, despite its many variants. In general, Roma also speak the dominant language of the region in which they live, or even several languages." *D.H. and Others v. Czech Republic*, Eur. Ct. Hum Rts. (Grand Chamber), Judgment of 13 November 2007, para. 12.

4. Ministry of Justice, *Statistics on Race and the Criminal Justice System–2006/7*, (London: Ministry of Justice, 2008)

5. Under Article 33 (2) a) of the Police Act an officer may take any person who cannot provide conclusive identification or who refuses to cooperate with police into short-term arrest of up to 12 hours or until his identity is verfied.

6. In Spain, the stop forms used nationality as a proxy for ethnicity. Each stop form noted the nationality on the identity document of the person stopped. In Girona the form also recorded

the officer's perception of ethnicity but the data analysis found that the two categories—officer's perception and nationality on the identity document—almost totally overlapped. Accordingly, for the sake of comparability, the analysis uses only the actual nationality as listed on the identity document. At this time, nationality is a feasible and reasonably accurate description of most minority residents (it does not capture Spanish Roma or *gitanos*) due to the recent nature of immigration to Spain and the fact that few migrants have Spanish nationality. The term "immigrant" and nationality-based descriptions are used throughout this report to refer to visible minorities in Spain. References to "Spaniards" refer to ethnic Spaniards. There are also significant numbers of white European migrants to Spain, particularly British citizens, but they are not resident in large numbers in the pilot site. See discussion of issues related to the selection of ethnic categories at Chapter V, section 3.

7   David Harris, *Profiles in Injustice: Why Racial Profiling Cannot Work*, (New York: The New Press, 2002). Joel Miller, Nick Bland, and Paul Quinton, *The Impact of Stops and Searches on Crime and the Community: Police Research Series Paper 127* (London: Home Office, 2000). Ronald Weitzer and Steven A. Tuch, "Determinants of Public Satisfaction with the Police" in *Police Quarterly* No. 8 (3) 2005.

8   These recommendations are complemented by boxes with specific lessons from the STEPSS project, described in Chapter IV.

9   In many European countries, identity checks are commonly part of each stop and search. For the sake of simplicity, in this report, we use the term "stops" throughout, regardless of whether the stop involves an identity check. Although under law, no police in the EU can stop a person solely to check their ID, in some cases the requirement for a reason—or "grounds"—for stops is so weak as to impose little or no restraint on officers in practice.

10 Centre for the Study of Democracy, Bulgaria; Professor András L. Pap and TÁRKI, Hungary; GEA21, Spain.

11 Open Society Justice Initiative, *"I Can Stop Whoever I Want;" Ethnic Profiling in Bulgaria, Hungary, and Spain,* (New York and Budapest: OSI, 2006).

12 Many European governments share a misperception that gathering ethnically-disaggregated data is prohibited by data protection norms. In fact, the European Racial Equality Directive explicitly recognizes the use of statistical data in order to demonstrate unequal treatment on the basis of race or ethnicity (EU Directive 2000/43/EC, Preamble, Para. 15), and European data protection law highlights the need to protect privacy and self-identification, while allowing for the good-faith collection and dissemination of ethnic data for legitimate purposes of public interest with certain safeguards in place.

13 Ministry of Justice, *Statistics on Race and the Criminal Justice System–2006/7*.

14 Research studies have questioned the accuracy of police recording of their stop activities and the degree to which the residential population data reflect the numbers of people living in an area versus the number of people "available" on the street where stops are taking place. In the areas studied, the available population tended to have a higher percentage of young people and people from ethnic minority groups. N.J. Bland, J. Miller et al. *Upping the PACE? An Evaluation of the Recommendations of the Stephen Lawrence Inquiry on Stops and Searches* (London: Home Office, 2000). MVA and J. Miller, *Profiling Populations Available for Stops and Searches.* (London: Home

Office, 2000). This study measured available populations through observational methods. The observed "available" population is then measured against the police records to determine disproportionality. Due to the cost of observational research, these studies tend to be snapshots of forces or areas. Thus, measures of disproportionality based on residential population remain an important and practical way of determining fairness in stop practices.

15 Ranges established by John Lamberth, U.S. statistician and expert on racial profiling. See www.lamberthconsulting.com.

16 John Lamberth, *Revised Statistical Analysis of the Incidence of Police Stops and Arrests of Black Drivers/Travellers on the New Jersey Turnpike between Intersection 1 and 3 from Years 1988 through 1991*. (*State v. Pedro Soto*, 734 A. 2d 350 N.J Super. Ct. Law. Div. 1996).

17 Figures cover the period April 1, 2006–April 1, 2007, and refer to stops and stop and searches conducted under Section 1 of the Police and Criminal Evidence Act 1984 (PACE). Stops conducted under other powers requiring no reasonable suspicion display even higher disproportionality. Ministry of Justice, *Statistics on Race and the Criminal Justice System–2006/7*.

18 Open Society Justice Initiative, *Ethnic Profiling in the Moscow Metro* (New York and Budapest: Open Society Justice Initiative, 2006), p. 31.

19 1990 Trust, *Stop and Search: The Views and Experiences of Black Communities on Complaining to the Police*. London: Metropolitan Police Authority, 2004. S. Havis and D. Best, *Stop and Search Complaints (2000–2001)*, (London: Police Complaints Authority, 2004).

20 Ministry of Justice, *Statistics on Race and the Criminal Justice System–2006/7*.

21 R. C. McCorkle, A. B. *500 Traffic Stop Data Collection Study - A Summary of Findings*. (Las Vegas: Office of the Attorney General of the State of Nevada, 2003).

22 Hit rates do not capture success in terms of charges and convictions. Research is limited, but one study of stop and search patterns in London found that only 40 percent of arrests following stops and searches resulted in a guilty verdict. J. Young, *Policing the Streets in London*, (Middlesex University: Centre for Criminology, 1994). Another U.K. study found that 50 percent of arrests from stops and searches resulted in a conviction, while 17 percent of arrests led to a caution. C. Philips and D. Brown, *Entry into the Criminal Justice System: A Survey of Police Arrest and their Outcomes*. Home office research study 185, (London: Home Office, 1989).

23 A U.K. study found that stops have a limited disruptive impact on overall crime, but there is little evidence of a deterrent effect. They note that intelligence may be an "added value" coming out of stops and searches but this is dependent on recording stops and searches and feeding the results into intelligence systems. J. Miller, N. Bland, and P. Quinton, *The Impact of Stops and Searches on Crime and the Community*, (London: Home Office, 2000).

24 Ministry of Justice, *Statistics on Race and the Criminal Justice System–2006/7*.

25 Eliot Spitzer, Attorney General of the State of New York, *The New York City Police Department's "Stop and Frisk" Practices: A Report to the People of the State of New York*, (New York: December 1999).

26 David A. Harris, *Profiles in Injustice: Why Racial Profiling Cannot Work*, (New York: The New Press, 2002).

27 For stops conducted under Section 1 of the 1984 Police and Criminal Evidence Act (PACE). Searches conducted under other powers (Section 60 of the Criminal Justice and Public Order Act 1994 or Section 44 of the Terrorism Act 2000) do not require reasonable suspicion.

28 M. FitzGerald, *Searches in London under Section 1 of the Police and Criminal Evidence Act 1984*, (London: Metropolitan Police Service, 1999).

29 Stops based on low discretion will still be influenced by officers' discretion as they will be called upon to interpret information and make judgements about who to stop.

30 P. Quinton, N. Bland, and J. Miller, *Police Stops, Decision-making and Practice*, (London: Home Office, 2000).

31 The Police and Criminal Evidence Act (PACE) 1984 Code of Practice A sets out the power of police to stop and search people on the street. Further powers to stop persons are set out in the Terrorism Act 2000 (Section 43 and Section 44) and Section 60 of the Criminal Justice and Public Order Act 1994.

32 Section 60 of the Criminal Justice and Public Order Act 1994 as amended by Section 8 of the Knives Act 1997 allows an inspector or higher ranked officer who reasonably fears serious violence or the carrying of weapons in a particular locality to authorize uniformed officers to search any person or vehicle in that locality for weapons for a period of 24 hours. Subsection 3 allows a superintendent to extend this authorization for a further 24 hours. Section 60 limits stops and searches to a specific time and place but does not require police to have any basis of reasonable suspicion.

33 *Ibid.*

34 M. FitzGerald, *Searches in London, under s1 of the Police and Criminal Evidence Act 1984*, (London: Metropolitan Police Service, 1999).

35 Ministry of Justice, *Statistics on Race and the Criminal Justice System–2006/7*, at pp. 24, 32.

36 Studies have questioned the quality of information entered on stop forms. A study in London found that officers repeatedly used uniform and standard phases to describe events, thereby undermining the requirement that suspicion be individualized. Almost all the forms had been initialled by a supervisor, thus supervisors were accepting search records presenting inadequate grounds of suspicion for stops and searches. Nacro, the crime prevention charity, *Policing Local Communities - The Tottenham Experiment*, (London: NACRO, 1997).

37 Eliot Spitzer, Attorney General of the State of New York, *The New York City Police Department's "Stop and Frisk" Practices: A Report to the People of the State of New York*, (December 1999).

38 The total population of Fuenlabrada is 209,102 of which 15.9 percent are foreigners (Funlabrada municipal government, July 17, 2008).

39 Hit rates are not calculated on the same grounds in all locations. In Fuenlabrada the "hit rate" includes all instances where the police discover a breach of the law (administrative and criminal) through their stops and/or searches. They do not include people caught in the act (*in flagrante*), though stops of persons in the act of committing offenses are included in the definition of positive outcomes in Girona, resulting in higher but non-comparable hit rates.

40 The "other" category in the Spanish data refers to all other nationalities combined.

41 They also included an open field to record "motivation" or actual suspicion leading to the stop. See discussion in this chapter on supervisors' use of this information.

42 It should be noted that hot spot operations are often designed to have a deterrent effect at that particular location. Deterrence is difficult to measure and may not show up in hit rates.

43 No arrests were made, as prostitution is not illegal in Spain.

44 It was not possible to analyze the number of repeat stops of the same women or to confirm that all stops took place in the industrial zone. Such data would illustrate how targeted the operation was in practice.

45 The operation was carried out in conjunction with the national police, as it was considered likely that there would be another bombing in Madrid due to the concurrence of two events: the trial of the March 11th bombing suspects and the hunger strike of the notable ETA member Iñaki de Juana Chaos.

46 The data generated by the municipal police and Mossos D'Esquadra was not analyzed until the end of project. Thus the project was unable to generate monthly reports on the trends emerging from the data for either police operational purposes or to share with the community during consultative meetings. Given the delay in analyzing the data, we are unable to explain the trend and patterns that emerge in as much detail as we would like.

47 Girona Municipal Police radio logs show that during the six months officers conducted 2170 stops; thus officers completed STEPSS forms in 70 percent of cases. The Mossos d'Esquadra initially reported that, compared to radio logs, they found that officers had completed forms in 70 percent of their stops. While falling short, the recording rate is high enough to support analysis. Shortly before going to print, Justice Initiative received aggregate numbers of stops by the Mossos d'Equadra in the Girona area recorded from radio logs; this showed that STEPSS captured just under 20 percent of the stops conducted. However, the aggregate number provided includes traffic stops—which were not included in STEPSS in Spain—including fixed check-points established on the national highway in response to terror and smuggling alerts. The Mossos data also include special units working in Girona that were not filling out STEPSS forms, and stops conducted at sporting events. The data cannot be disaggregated, but it provides reason to believe that the compliance rate of Mossos officers in the STEPSS project may in fact have been significantly under 70 percent. The data must be read as, at best, a general reflection of practice.

48 Positive results include all administrative and criminal offenses, and persons detained in the commission of a crime or misdemeanor. This is a broader definition than that used in Fuenlabrada, which accounts in some measure for the higher hit rate in the Girona data.

49 Population data from the Girona municipal government, "Age data by nationality and gender" July 23, 2008. Girona also has a significant commuter and transient population who come from the surrounding area for shopping and entertainment. The analysis refers to the four most stopped groups in Girona and an "other" group including all other foreign groups (whose population numbers were too small to be statistically significant).

50 While the hit rate for Romanians is higher, it is important to note that the number of stops and arrests is low and more data would be necessary to verify whether this hit rate remained high and could be associated with offending rates.

51 The criteria established by each force for what counts as "directed" and "non-directed" differ substantially.

52 Stops in Hungary are not limited to discretionary stops on the street of those suspected of committing a crime, but also include identity checks of people who witness or report crimes. Stop numbers have been adjusted to remove the ID checks that are performed on people who report or witness crimes. The police provided the estimated proportions of these ID checks at 10 percent in Kaposvár, 20 percent in Szeged and 30 percent in Budapest. The total number of stops was calculated using records of radio logs kept by police headquarters in each area. Data collection methords differed across pilot sites: in some areas officers are required to call in to check if someone is wanted, while in other areas stops are recorded on daily activity logs.

53 The Budapest Sixth District Police Unit covers an inner-city area with one of the city's three main railway stations, a large shopping area, offices, and restaurants. There is a small residential population and large commuter and transient population. The census population is 39,000 but we use a figure of 65,000 in the analysis to reflect the large transient population, based on a calculation by Zsolt Akács, head of the Department for Public Order, Sixth District.

54 Population of the Greater Kaposvár Region. Source: KSH Népességtudományi Kutató Intézet, Előreszámítási adatbázis, 2003 (http://www.nepinfo.hu/index.php?m=830&id=566).

55 Population of the Greater Szeged Region. Source: http://www.icicom.hu/teruletfo/csmhu15.htm.

56 Under Article 33 (2) a) of the Police Act an officer may take any person who cannot provide conclusive identification or who refuses to cooperate with police into short-term arrest of up to 12 hours or until their identity is verfied.

57 Act LXIX of 1999 on Petty Offenses (Petty Offenses Act) establishes petty offenses ranging from "grave," or those punishable by a 60-day prison term (e.g., prostitution or physical threats), to those punishable by fines (e.g., petty theft or traffic infractions).

58 If stops related to traffic offenses are removed, the remaining stops result in one percent arrest, three percent short-term arrest, 19 percent petty offense procedure, and 76 percent no further action taken.

59 ID checks were considered "unsatisfactory" by the project team if they failed to reach a level of specificity needed to reconstruct the perceived suspicion on the basis of information provided by the office.

60 Roma ethnicity is based on the perception of the officer making the stop; Hungarian forms recorded officer perception of ethnicity. See Chapter V, section 4 for a discussion of stop form design.

61 László Hablicsek, Márta Gyenei, István Kemény, *Kísérleti számítások a roma lakosság területi jellemzőinek alakulására és 2021-ig történő előrebecslésére*, p. 63. See: http://www.nepinfo.hu/index.php?p=605&m=1003.

62 István Kemény: *A magyarországi cigány népesség demográfiája*: http://www.demografia.hu/Demografia/2004_3-4/Kemenypercent20Istvan_kozl.pdf.

63 Disproportionality ratios are calculated on the basis of estimated Roma populations. The 2008 Roma population of Budapest is estimated at around 75,000 or 4.4 percent of the total popula-

tion of 1.7 million. Due to local population concentration, Roma make up a higher percentage of the population of the Sixth District and its vicinity, but are not above 10 percent of the local population; this higher estimate is used in calculating disproportionality. The Szeged Roma population estimate was calculated by László Zélity, head of the Szeged Police Headquarters; the Kaposvár population estimate was calculated by Imré Bogdán, president of the Kaposvár Roma Self-government.

64 Data entry took some 15 minutes per form due to deficient training (e.g., officers were not told to use the TAB button on the Numeric Pad for greater speed and did not have touch typing skills). The evaluation team was told of some extreme cases when officers spent three to five hours in a single day entering stop form data.

65 Policy audits are a fairly common tool that is valuable for determining policies and practices. They can also get police management thinking about actual practice—what is happening at street level—and how it may diverge from official policy. Policy audits should use a range of materials beyond law, policies, statistics and qualitative information—such as media reports, interviews with local community members, and complaints.

66 The guidance for this assessment was prepared based on inputs from the United Kingdom's Ministry of Justice and through consultation with other experts and then adapted to fit each local context. Further information is available in the STEPSS resource packet which can be obtained from the Justice Initiative by emailing a request to info@justiceinitiative.org.

67 Prior to the project, Bulgarian police were required to complete up to five forms when they conducted a stop. In a compromise, the police added other details to the basic STEPSS form that were not specifically related to the objectives of the project, with the aim of testing whether one form could replace all of the other documents. This created problems during the pilot, because the stop form did not replace the other forms and so created added paperwork.

68 1990 Trust, *Stop and Search: The Views and Experiences of Black Communities on Complaining to the Police*. London: Metropolitan Police Authority, 2004. S. Havis and D. Best, *Stop and Search Complaints (2000–2001)*, (London: Police Complaints Authority, 2004).

69 STEPSS used paper forms, but other approaches to data collection are equally valid. The critical elements of the process are the data collected, and providing the person stopped with some form of receipt. In some U.S. jurisdictions, police call information in to radio dispatchers; it is also possible to give the person stopped a business card with information on the officer and a unique reference number to enable citizen complaints.

70 In the United Kingdom, for example, the categorization used for immigrants from the Caribbean has evolved from "colored," through West Indian, black, Afro-Caribbean, and African-Caribbean, to black British in the space of 50 years. The United Kingdom will review and may change these and other categories again at the next census to reflect population changes with growing European migration. There is also currently a debate around recording religion.

71 Sample operational guidance, like other STEPSS materials, are included in a STEPSS resource packet, available from the Justice Initiative by emailing a request to info@justiceinitiative.org.

72 A Harvard study on the impact of diversity training in addressing discrimination in the workplace found that it has no effect or even adverse effects. Frank Dobbin, Alexandra Kalev, and

Erin Kelly, "Best Practices or Best Guesses? Assessing the Efficacy of Corporate Affirmative Action and Diversity Policies," *American Sociological Review*, Vol. 71, No. 4, August 2006, 589–617.

73 The community trainers were of immigrant origin, but all worked with various local and regional NGOs, including Centro UNESCO and were experienced trainers.

74 Sample forms are included in the STEPSS resource packet, available from the Justice Initiative by emailing a request to info@justiceinitiative.org.

75 The Justice Initiative STEPSS project managers distributed extensive materials from the British police, including introductions to and discussions of data analysis. These materials were reviewed at a data analysis meeting held in February 2007 in Budapest. In retrospect, it appears that the novelty of the analysis for partners in the pilot country settings would have been better served by preparing a special introduction and step-by-step guidance. Justice Initiative has prepared a "stops monitoring tool" providing a basic introduction to stop data analysis which is available in the STEPSS resource packet.

76 U.K. and U.S. research shows that unsatisfactory police-public contact has a negative impact on public confidence in police, not only for the individual directly involved, but also for their family, friends and associates. Joel Miller, Nick Bland and Paul Quinton (2000) *The Impact of Stops and Searches on Crime and the Community* Police Research Series Paper 127 London: Home Office; Ronald Weitzer and Steven A. Tuch "Determinants of Public Satisfaction with the Police" in *Police Quarterly* No. 8 (3) 2005: 279-297; Joel Miller, Robert C. Davis, Nicole J. Henderson, John Markovic and Christopher W. Ortiz (2004) *Public opinions of the police: The influence of friends, family, and media*. NIJ technical report (2001-IJ-CX-0038); Dennis P. Rosenbaum, Amie M. Schuck, Sandra K. Costello, Darnell F. Hawkins, and Marianne K. Ring "Attitudes toward the police: The effects of direct and vicarious experience" Police Quarterly No. 8 (3) 2005: 343-365. Research also demonstrates that bad treatment by the police is associated with reduced cooperation with the police. McCluskey, John D., Stephen D. Mastrofski, and Roger B. Parks. 1999. "To acquiesce or rebel: Predicting citizen compliance with police requests," *Police Quarterly* 2:389–416.

77 Studies in both the U.K. and U.S. show unambiguously that regular community consultation contributes directly to reducing crime and improving the public's sense of security. David Weisburd and John E. Eck, "What Can Police Do to Prevent Crime, Disorder and Fear," in *The Annals of the American Academy of Political and Social Science* (2004, Vol. 593, No. 1, 42–65); David A. Harris, *Profiles in Injustice: Why Racial Profiling Cannot Work* (New York: New Press, 2002); Rachel Tuffin, Julia Morris, and Alexis Poole *An Evaluation of the Impact of the National Reassurance Policing Programme* (London: Home Office, 2006).

78 The legal standards governing police powers in Bulgaria are outlined in the Law on the Ministry of Interior (LMOI) and the Regulation on its Implementation (RILMOI): LMOI effective 01.05.2006; promulgated SG No. 17 of February 24, 2006; amended SG No. 30 of April 11, 2006; amended SG No. 102 of December 19, 2006. RILMOI promulgated SG No. 47 of June 9, 2006.

79 Law of the Ministry of the Interior (LMOI), Instruction I-23, p. 24, Chapter 4, Part 1, art. 57(1).

80 Ibid., art. 57(2).

81 Act XXXIV of 1994 on police (hereafter Police Act), amended text effective from 1st January 2008.

82 Article 33 (2) a) of the Police Act: In order to protect public security, the police officer may bring to the authority or other competent organisation any person who cannot identify him/herself in a conclusive manner or refuses to identify him/herself when requested to do so by the police officer.

83 Article 38 (1) of the Police Act.

84 Article 29 (1) of the Police Act.

85 Article 44 (b) of the Police Act.

86 Article 20 (2) of the Police Act.

87 Article 70/A of Act XX of the 1949 Constitution of the Republic of Hungary.

88 Decision no. 61 of 1992, date of passage November 20, 1992.

89 Article 13 (2) of the Police Act.

90 Article 2 (1) of the Police Act.

91 Decision No. 32/1991 (January 28, 1991), Constitutional Court of Spain.

92 Decision No. 4005/1991 (April 15, 1993), Supreme Court of Spain.

93 Organic Law 2/1986, March 13, 1986, of the Security Forces and Bodies.

94 The Spanish Supreme Court upheld the legality of a decision by the national police to stop an African-American woman with Spanish citizenship solely on the grounds of her race. See *Rosalind Williams*, Spanish Constitutional Court Decision No. 13/2001, January 29, 2001 (STC 13/2001).

95 PACE 2008: para 2.2.

96 The PACE Code of Practice was last updated on December 31, 2008. The code makes a distinction between "stop and accounts," where people are stopped and asked to account for their actions, and stops that lead to searches. Police are no longer required to record information on "stop and accounts" other than the ethnicity of the person stopped.

97 Information from the police units participating in the project. The three concerned headquarters collected the information on the total number of ID checks in different ways. The Sixth District collected the information from the register of database inquiries (in terms of internal norms, all ID checked people shall be checked in the central database for wanted persons, so from the number of inquiries initiated into this database, the number of checks can be calculated). The other two headquarters provided the information based on the daily reports of officers on duty, with the database summarizing the data coming from these daily reports.